MIGRATIONS

Poetry & Prose for Life's Transitions

edited by Sheila Packa

Wildwood River Press
Duluth, Minnesota
2011

Cover art and design by Kathy McTavish. Printed in the United States.

ISBN: 978-0-9843777-3-2

Library of Congress Control Number: 2011935069

Wildwood River Press
1748 Wildwood Road
Duluth, MN 55804
www.wildwoodriver.com

ACKNOWLEDGMENTS

I want to thank the many people that have been involved in the poetry groups
and workshops of the Community Arts Learning Project. I am grateful for the
wonderful support that I've received from the Duluth Poet Laureate program
sponsored by Lake Superior Writers, the Zeppa Family Foundation, the Duluth
Public Arts Commission, UMD English Department, UMD Academic Affairs,
UMD College of Liberal Arts, the College of St. Scholastica English Department,
Lake Superior College, Friends of the Duluth Public Library, Arrowhead Reading
Council, and Barnes & Noble Booksellers. Thank you to Kathy and Janet McTa-
vish. Thank you to the Northern Lakes Food Bank. Also, thank you to the staff at
the Safe Haven Shelter for Women, the Family Justice Center, and the Domestic
Abuse Intervention Programs for providing a room with a table to a poet.

This activity is funded in part by the Arrowhead Regional Arts Council with
money from the Minnesota Arts and Cultural Heritage fund as appropriated by
the Minnesota State Legislature with money from the vote of the people of Minne-
sota on November 4, 2008.

Whatever keeps you from your work
becomes your work.
                    — *Carolyn Forché*

CONTENTS

INTRODUCTION
Sheila Packa

Each fall, along the western shore of Lake Superior, hundreds of thousands of migrating birds ride the thermal currents above the dark conifers and bright reds and golds of autumn leaves. They follow the shoreline. Under their outstretched wings, I reach for the language of flight as I gather and arrange this collection of poems and prose.

This book is about migrations in life that all of us make: the embarking, the long journey, the returning — beginnings and endings, irrevocable. We are like birds in migration, traveling between memory and new beginnings. The stories and poems capture the voices of many writers and the landscape of the North and of Lake Superior.

It's a common story, migration. My grandparents were Finnish immigrants who arrived in the U.S. in the early part of the 20th century and homesteaded in northern Minnesota. English was difficult to learn. Their life was difficult. The growing season was short. My mother didn't spend much time talking about the hard times. After all, it was the good times that got her through — love, music and dancing. I've made many changes in my own life. Each poem or story here captures a moment of change. These changes range from having a baby to losing a loved one. Some are about moving through violence, relationship break-ups, illness, growing up and aging.

In nature, we live among deep patterns: migrations, erosions, rivers, storms, seasons. Our lives have these patterns, ever-changing like the forest and land. Good writing is grounded in the body and in the landscape. Good stories and poems, engaging the five senses of the body, reveal the weight of things as well as the beauty.

I hope this collection will build community. Art and writing help us to know patterns, natural or mythic. Artistic work brings a sense of immediacy, a disturbing familiarity, and a location in strange beauty. It translates into vision.

This collection brings together two projects. As poet laureate of Duluth, I've invited people in the community to write about life's transitions and to write odes for each other. In mind was a Mexican custom in some families to seek blessings from the matriarch. If you ask for a blessing, she is honor bound to provide one. This is especially important during times of transition: a loss or a death, an illness, a recovery, departure, journey, deployment, marriage, new job, new home, a birth, a new beginning.

In the first project, I collected work from area writers and made placemats to be distributed at the Empty Bowl fundraiser by the Northern Lakes Food Bank. It was my goal to distribute these to area social service organizations: hospice programs, the Women's Shelter, the Food Shelf, Detox, and other organizations that assist homeless or hungry people.

In the second project, funded by an Arts and Cultural Heritage Community Arts Learning grant, I partnered with the Domestic Abuse Intervention Programs, the Women's Shelter and the Family Justice Center to offer workshops and weekly writing sessions for people moving through violence. Inspired by a "Writing Is My Shelter" program, I asked friends to donate unused journals that I gave to people attending the writing sessions. In a writing group or alone, the page offers a place to put the things that are difficult to bear; once on paper, one can shift roles from victim or witness to one that is more active. Writing puts one in charge of the story. Psychologically, the change is profound. Our story is an internal map that we use to travel through life.

In every workshop, I hear new and arresting voices. I've included poems of blessing and transition, polished and unpolished, that capture an image, a turning point, and a unique voice. Each was like a bird inside a larger flock and as such, wide-ranging. They are alphabetized according to first name instead of last name, suggesting an intimate, less formal gathering. I like beginning with Alissa Tran's Ode to Air. The title pays homage to poet Pablo Neruda. The last poem by Yvonne Rutford makes a physically satisfying end. In between are many journeys and flights.

Years ago, in the Split Rock Arts Program, I talked with poet Carolyn Forché about the difficulty of finding time to write. It seemed I was always in transition, juggling many responsibilities, and found it challenging to set aside enough time.

"Whatever keeps you from your work becomes your work," she said, meaning that I should write about what I was currently grappling with. Along with her husband, freelance photographer, Harry Mattison, she had facilitated the Iron Range Documentation Project. As a social activist and witness to atrocity, Carolyn Forché's own voice became the vehicle of many, and she wrote to reveal the pain and suffering in Nicaragua and other places. Later, she edited an anthology, *Against Forgetting: Twentieth Century Poetry of Witness* (W.W. Norton, 1993).

Poetry can be many things: song, story, memoir, philosophy, image. Poetry can use many narrative strategies: journey, list, prayer, blessing, letter, or quest. Poetry can witness; it can be an agent of change. It can preserve a moment with vivid immediacy. It can awaken. Its purpose is diverse, but it always illuminates.

I followed Forché's advice, and now give that same advice to a lot of writers. If something is an obstacle, write about it. If something is getting in the way of your writing, then you should be writing about that. If you are preoccupied, let your thoughts go into ink on a page.

It is important to create a time and place for writing. There is evidence that keeping a journal improves one's health and immunity, and that it speeds recovery from illness. Writing is a tool of the mind, but I also think it is a tool of the soul. The poet Linda Hogan once said, "Whatever you write will make it stronger." Writing helps one find and use a voice. Writing strengthens identity and allows it to develop and change. Writing about place helps us understand our roots and name our desires, not just for ourselves but for the larger world.

A community that honors and celebrates the arts becomes a community of openness and exchange. Unique voices rise that bring images and stories that stir us. The arts foster diversity not uniformity. The community that invests in the activity of art making is preserving its culture and promoting creativity. We are all strengthened.

These poems, stories and essays form a conversation; I invite the reader to participate. At this moment, something is changing in your life. Find an image or a metaphor to enter the complexity. For me, writing is a type of way-finding, a lamp in darkness.

— Sheila Packa, *September, 2011*

ODE TO AIR
Alissa Tran

Why do you have to do that?

Sing so softly into my being in the evening?

Assault me with a new fragrance along the sidewalk passing

Gardens, houses, dogs, birds, and the lake

Along the way?

Why do you have to remind me and catch in my windpipe

Every time I hold on to a serving of your lung filling a void a little too long?

Sometimes when you linger there I wonder where have you been.

Perhaps yesterday you were sharing space with that dark-eyed young man scowling at me across the aisle on the city bus.

Perhaps you have been drifting and just get wistful of all the places you have been and I can be so boring always watching the door.

I have no time for you and your rush into my nostril, your silence on my lips. Please leave me alone.

Oh, you are you say. I am already alone. Alone in oneness you say.

Very funny, stop bothering me, I am watching the door, working on emptiness.

Stop waiting for me then, to be absorbed into your perfection, your complicit stillness.

I am waiting to feel like I belong here, as if I could join in.
You keep inviting yourself in like that and I am going to lock the door.
Deadbolt.

Understand. I don't have time for lilac, smog, mist, wet dogs, sticky children, or any other perfumes you bring my way. I am looking for the zipper on my body bag.

But, oh, air. You are ever so patiently leaning into my throat, pressing in around my diaphragm in a yawn. You are near and far at once, touching all of my beloved objects, people, space.

Oh, air, why do you have to be so sweet as to include me when I don't even remember to bring you in from the cold freezing the mucus membrane and my wet hair in the wind?

Why do you have to be so constant, so ready to absorb me in your directions, seasons and life? Why do you love so unconditionally when no one notices you much at all?

Thank you air for bringing me here, for stirring the dust and seasonings, the fibers and thoroughfares of my being and patterning.

Thank you for whistling with my lost loved ones and making me more aware. For waking me up. For being so fair. For following the sunset and still remaining here.

For traveling to the moon and back and to infinity and perhaps at one time doing the same for some other being, a raven, maybe or an alien in another galaxy where all my dreams drift through.

Thank you for bringing us together to dance and to frolic, to swim and play, to teach and listen as you pass and transform in, around, through everything.

Why do you have to do that air? Allow me to walk away from this door I have been pressing my nose against. For mixing with anesthesia and allowing me to understand that the ashes, cologne, water table, cycles of my life are present in this moment.

For helping me to see that you have been my constant friend and you contain so much. That one day I will join you in another capacity but today I can rise with the wind of my soul and not wait any longer.

2

GIVE PEACE TO KENYA: LOVE POEM
Alissa Tran

Let me be the sun at your back

The smile at your mother's door

The red tea you hold on your tongue

The fruit of your childhood's noon

Hear the laughter of your kin inside me

Let me be the flesh of your own heart

And the rhythm of a nearby village

I will be the dust on the road to Nairobi

And the kindness of strangers in her streets

I will be the turquoise that bathes you

On the hilltop of your countryside

When you gaze into my eyes

See your ocean

Let me love like this

When you greet me

Come with a holy kiss

Let me remind your memory

Give peace to Kenya

DIVIDED

Amy Jo Swing

The north side of the river is still
holding onto its trees' leaves — coppery
oaks, yellow birch and popple, the orange
and red spectrum are mostly blown away though
nothing like the river's south side, which is
stick bare and color palette brown. There's
a bit of panic now that the anticipation of
color is gone. Now that the drive home is dark,
color only memory, and even shape is suspect.

HAPPY BIRTHDAY
Audrey L'Amie

Your day comes
as I sit
with a Coke
and think of bills,
of garbage,
of flour mites
I baked into bread.

But you wait
to arrive
until after I rise
to brush mascara
and dress your brother
who cries, half awake,
in wet pajamas.

We travel in a car
without brakes
to the hospital
that welcomes not at all
two children,
with a child,
having a child.

It is time
to push and heave
to wrench, to move
your nine pounds through,
and I feel
in the cavity
that once pumped emotion,
a rush
of scarlet intuition:

I know that soon
and later
and forever
it will be

me
who serves the King,
your brother,
you.

And while I strain,
I listen
to men talk
of chainsaws and trees,
as they sit,
enwrapped and rapt,
one in white
the other in black.

And I know,
as I twist and pull
at metal grips
instead of a hand,
how little
and little
of me remains,
how my quality
degrades
with the brakes
of our car.

Now, the final count;
your cry flies,
indignant,
from walls of tiles,
and I feel
the weight of years
yet to be,
bearing
unceasing
pleas and please.

XANADU
Bernadette Savage

Let's meet at the house of Zen
and fly to our castle in the air.
Let's romp in the clouds and feel
pebbly drops of rain on our skin.
Let's be overzealous about everything —
gamble and eat whatever we have a yen for.
Let's banish all zealots
with our long jaded fingers —
and when vertigo threatens our existence
we'll attach ourselves to a celestial star.

THESE DOORS
Bernadette Savage

YOU ARE IN MY THOUGHTS
ARE WITH YOU ARE PART OF
MY UNIVERSAL GOD IS LIKE
A RIVER TOO WIDE TO CROSS
TO BEAR IT NO LONGER THAN
SPRING TIME ARE YOU WILL BE
IN MY EVERY PRAYER FOR WE
SING WITH THE FULLNESS OF
JOY IN THE WORLD OF THE
MEEK FOR THEY SHALL INHERIT
THE EARTH MOTHER SUPERIOR
SHINING BIG SEA WATER CAN
WASH AWAY ALL OUR SINS
OF THE FATHER ARE VISITED
UPON THE SUN GROWS FLOWERS
THAT CUT THROUGH THE
NEGATIVE CHARGE WHICH
IS HOOKED UP LAST NIGHT
I SAW A GHOST OF A CHANCE
TO MAKE IT THROUGH THESE
DOORS ARE ALWAYS OPEN

IN AFRICA
Bernadette Savage

The Honeyguide bird shows the badger to the honeycomb.
He cracks it open with his strong claws. They feed together
and do not speak.

You have shared your children with me
and they call out, "Grammie — you're here."
I savor their sweetness like honey on a spoon.

Cancer has brought us suffering and heaviness.
We sit at the intake table of Hope Lodge
and do not speak.

They want to know what medications you are on.
What I know is this: right now you want me
to move away from you.

I can do that. You have looked for safety with Jesus,
and now I must get my own room. But I am still the bird
and you the badger.

We talk about radiation and your husband, kids, work.
Before I go to my room and bend to kiss you goodbye,
I smell your skin, the same as when you were a baby.

Your neck is turning black from radiation; your eyes say —
you cannot help me now.

BY THE DOOR ON A BAR ROOM WALL
Bev Berntson

By the door on a bar room wall
positioned for all to see,
hangs a sign, a proclamation, a post
or is it really a plea?

Jade Has Farm Fresh Eggs

In letters black and oh, so bold
the words so straight and plain,
my exit is arrested as I wonder
is this profane?

No doubt Jade's eggs are healthy,
she's clearly a country chick,
but that sign leaves me hoping
this isn't her only trick.

It's hard to scratch a living
from bedrock, sweat, and soil,
but does she know that trading her yoke
isn't worth that kind of toil?

Living in the country can be lonely
and if it's company she desires,
shouldn't she find a young Cock-a-Doodle-Doo
before her fertility expires?

Oh, cooped-up girl with hardened shell
you have my sympathy.
I hope you find some better employ
before you're no longer cage-free.

MEMORIES OF MY FATHER
Beverly Hanks

When I was three years old back in 1936 during the deep depression, my father was a foreman of a construction company. He was laid off two weeks before Christmas and was seeking but couldn't find work. One day, not long before Christmas, he received a letter in the mail from a friend who was a farmer in Wisconsin. He wanted my father to come down and do some dynamite blasting, because he knew my father was experienced in that line of work. It was a dangerous job and the farmer couldn't find anyone that was willing to take the job. He wanted my father to come right away.

In preparation for the trip, my mother packed him plenty of food and extra wool socks because it was cold and he would have to walk the journey to Wisconsin. He recently sold his car and his only way to get there was on foot. The farmer lived thirty miles away. My father would stop and rest and visit farms along the way because he knew them from previous work in the area and he knew he would be welcome. He made it to the blasting job and it turned out well. He began his trek home. My mother was anxious because the weather was cold and it had started to snow.

On the eighth day of his trip, I was looking out the window and saw someone coming up the road. It was snowing heavily. When he passed the streetlight I realized it was my father. I yelled down to my mother, excited to give her the news. My mother was joyous and relieved that he made it home safely, and just in time for Christmas. When he came in the door, he grabbed both of us and hugged us at the same time. Then he opened his pack and gave me some of his wool socks. I was puzzled, but when I looked, there were oranges in them. This was a special treat. Oranges were very hard to find and were my favorite fruit. I will never forget this memorable Christmas and how thankful we were to have my father home.

POEM ON MY BIRTHDAY
Bonita Sutliff

I've climbed the butte
warm in the sun
above the tunnel
and winding road.

How deep the sky
and white the clouds
above red rock
breeze swept clean.

Other buttes are less distant
and a river threads below.

NIGHT BRINGS
Brooke Ballavance

Night comes. She drapes her deep black cape over the sky
She comes to put the sun to sleep
Then brings the moon out to start the night
With the moon come the stars
The stars come out one by one
A lone owl calls out as if to say Night has come
Night brings out the creatures of the dark
Wake up for it is soon to be light
Once Night is done her sister Morning Light is slowly making her way
To tell Night that it is time for her to go
Sleep until the time comes for her to come back
Night has gone now
She has left her sister Dawn behind

MORE THAN THAT
Bud Brand

More than just bifocal glasses
   on a pair of failing eyes,
more than just a hearing aid
   that is impossible to disguise,
more than just a walking stick
   that provides another leg,
more than Social Security checks
   that forbid the need to beg,
more than just a rocking chair
   that's used to waste the days,
more than just a sullen face
   with a stone-like silent gaze;
yes, more than that are twinkling eyes
   as bright as any star,
yes, more than that is a sparkling smile —
   the best around by far,
yes, more than that is the voice of wisdom
   from the lips of a knowing sage,
yes, more than that is a wealth of experience
   that only comes with age,
yes, more than that is a helping hand
   and a shoulder on which to lean,
yes, more than that is a work of art...
   for that is a fellow human being.

MIGRACIÓN - MIGRATION
Cecilia Ramón

When I think about December 1994, the summer when I left Buenos Aires...the country where I was born...I see the suitcase laying open in my room for days...not knowing what to take, what to leave behind...

how could I have known that after the departure there would be no arrival but always a thin veil, a distance, a synonym, never the right gesture or the precise word...

a new freedom in the constant translation...my sister for ever far, wrapped in our mother tongue...and myself always reaching...but arriving?

Julio Cortázar's words always with me...Se puede partir de cualquier cosa / one can depart from anything, una caja de fósforos / a matchbox, un golpe de viento en el tejado / a gust of wind on the roof, el estudio número 3 de Scriabin / Scriabin's Etude #3, un grito allá abajo en la calle / a scream in the street...

el riesgo está en eso / the risk is exactly that, en que se puede partir de cualquier cosa pero después hay que llegar / one can depart from anything but then one has to arrive...

arrive? how? to where? with whom?

EMERGENCE
Cindy Spillers

Tenacious crocus
Erupts through frozen darkness.
No turning back now.

LONG NIGHTS
Connie Wanek

> *It's good to have poems that begin with tea and end with God.*
> — *Robert Bly*

A cup forgotten on the windowsill,
half full of cold tea, half of moonlight.
The rocking chair sits alone now,
its back erect and its seat ample.
There I nursed the first baby, and read
The Alexandria Quartet, wherein
a child was a further romance.
I still feel her in my arms, limp with sleep,
and see her heartbeat in her fontanel.
Whenever I tried to lay her in her crib
her eyes flew open. Let her cry, they said.
But I never let her cry.

My mother carried six of us,
one after the other, on her hip,
as we descended from her embrace
to our stations on the earth. She says
to this day her left hip is higher,
her left arm brutally strong,
her right infinitely dexterous.
Long were the nights she spent in labor
wrestling babies from the Creator.

THE MIDWIFE
Connie Wanek

She was a medium, a fortune teller,
or an emissary sent to God himself
to beg humbly that the child
come whole and sound
and soon. Her hands were so clean,
the nails clipped or bitten,
the skin dry and tight.
She slept off and on,
accustomed to resting when she could
in a bed or chair,
like a traveler crossing the frontier
between tragedy and comedy,
land forever claimed by both sides.
What she witnessed
was the opposite of drowning,
a reenactment of the moment
the first amphibian took a breath,
the tadpole of a child
swimming eagerly into her hands.

PUMPKIN
Connie Wanek

> *None is so poor that he need sit on a pumpkin. — Thoreau*

To write as a field grows pumpkins,
to scribble page after page with an orange crayon,
to lose teeth and still smile,
to survive a frost that blackened acres,
to wake after surgery.

To live without rotting from within,
to ignore imperfections of the skin,
to be heavy, and still be chosen,
to please a strict vegetarian,
to end the day full of light.

HONEY
Connie Wanek

Luxury itself, thick as a Persian carpet,
honey fills the jar
with the concentrated sweetness
of countless thefts,
the blossoms bereft, the hive destitute.

Though my debts are heavy
honey would pay them all.
Honey heals, honey mends.
A spoon takes more than it can hold
without reproach. A knife plunges deep,
but does no injury.

Honey moves with intense deliberation.
Between one drop and the next
forty lean years pass in a distant desert.
What one generation labored for
another receives,
and yet another gives thanks.

BLESSINGS
Deborah Cooper

May you be blessed with a spirit of gentleness,
a heart that is tender.

May you be blessed with a spirit of strength
shining within you.

May you be blessed with a spirit of compassion,
a fervent caring.

May you be blessed with a spirit of courage
daring to be who you are.

May you be blessed by
    the friend around the corner
    & the friend ten thousand miles away...

    the velocity of love,
    crossing all borders...

    the myriad of ways
    the missing stay with us.

May the earth hold you.
May the wind lift you ever up.
May the fire draw and warm you.
May the water quench and soothe your soul.

A STIRRING
Deborah Cooper

The house you live in
is the house at the edge
of the woods.

You are forever looking out.

The woods are made of light
and shadow

the trees
toss the breeze
to one another

toss the birds
into the sky

always, a stirring
in the underbrush.

In the night
the trees are hung with stars

and you can hear the owl
wonder

as you wonder

some nights,
the keening of the wolves...

you understand this too.

Mornings,
tea warming your hands,
you stand at the window

and watch the day begin

and every morning
there is something new.

You will not turn away
until you've found it
or until it has found you.

All night, you dream
you move into the woods,
taking only what you'll need

a sack of apples
and a candle
and a quilt

a pen,
a book of empty pages.

POTTERY AND POETRY
Diane Dinndorf Friebe

Throw the clay down
Center it
Pedal
Keep the wheel moving
Hold your hands to the clay
Smoothly, steadily
Pulling the shape from the earth
Watching the clay rise up
Circling round and round
As your fingers create
Hollowing out a center with your thumbs
Holding the clay, the concept
Creative life flowing
Unnoticed but strong
Hands and pot one
Hands disappearing into clay
Clay into hands
Adjusting your fingers
To shape the vase
Slowing
Feeling it finishing itself

Throw the words down
Center them
Open your mind
Keep the thoughts moving
Hold the pen to the idea
Smoothly, steadily
Pulling the shape from the earth
Watching the poem rise up
Circling round and round
As your hands create
Hollowing out a theme with the ink
Tacking down details
Creative life flowing
Unnoticed but strong
Hands and poem one
Hands disappearing into letters

Letters into hands
Changing your thoughts
To edit the poem
Slowing
Feeling it finishing itself

THIS POEM
Ellie Schoenfeld

This poem
is a little paper boat
floating in a river full
of moonlight and undulating fish
slowly making its way
to you.
This poem
is the breath held
in a room lit only
by cakelight,
in those moments
before the wish is made,
before the candles go dark
and tendrils of buoyant smoke
float up into the stratosphere
and into your lungs
and become the wish
which was always you.
This poem
is your fondest wish coming true.

This poem
dances through the ethers
in three-quarter time
to waltz with you
on a rainy night.
This poem
is a blanket
that covers you.
This poem
is an origami bird
carefully folded and gliding
into your sleep
where you are having
a sweet dream
about floating
in a little paper boat
while under the water
iridescent fish
tremble in the moonlight.

WE HAVE NO IDEA
Ellie Schoenfeld

We wander in the Spring
through the uncountable shades of green,
slightly lost.
We open our mouths
and turtles leap
into the watery ditches.

We try to sing
but all our mouths want
to do is kiss.

We have no idea
what the sun will
call back to life,
his warm fingers digging deep
into the winter
which is melting away
inside of us.
Elemental songs reach
the sleeping bear
who is dreaming about a time
filled with every kind
of fruit and berry,
delicious and dripping,
the scent sliding sweet
under the nostrils,
across the soul.

What has been asleep
is waking up.

Bird songs waft
between our blood cells.
Somewhere a nest
is holding something
about to hatch.

We open our mouths to see
what will happen next.

We move
from one kind of green
to another
just wanting
to taste everything.

WHAT I SEND YOU
Ellie Schoenfeld

I send you
this flock of birds
and every dream harbored
under every feather.

I send you this cloud
that dreams of the beach
and looks like a horse galloping hard.

I send you this
quiet field filled
with people asleep
under the ground
who are dreaming about us,
dreaming our lives
into being.

I send you
the very first poem —
the original result
of mixing breathing
with the beating of a heart,
mystery made manifest.
Between the storm
and your skin
there will always be
this poem.

ANOTHER SEASON
Felicia Schneiderhan

In the final weeks
I sleep late, lie in bed in the afternoons,
Read and watch the Mountain Ash berries
Fall from the tree outside our window.
Freed by their own weight,
Or plucked by finches and robins.
Last year's goods gone to make room for
New shoots and leaves.

The world blossoms into the colors of spring,
Purple and red and the white promises of apples.

Beyond the shore a ship
Bellows to the lift bridge,
Their conversation carried to me by late fog, swelling on the sidewalks,
Trailing the postman, the dog walker at lunch.
The garden is weeded, wisteria waiting to wind the fence.
We are waiting to meet someone we don't know.

He is late.
After the solstice the cinching starts, the quavering, the pull.
I lie in the hospital bed, watching a salty
Glide to the bridge, to port.
Where has it been? What lies in its hull?
I breathe, and brace, and listen to my husband's voice,
Marking time in the last mile.

We carry him home,
Through the backyard muddled by
Small beads of hard, green apples.
I think back to fall, to the heavy scent of too-ripe apples,
Filling buckets in the pantry.
This year there will be more, and the next.
Every year, another season of fruit.

He has only just arrived.
Already, I see him going.

CONSIDER PA LING
Francine Sterle

Under a pale veil of moonlight
      A white horse
            Enters the white flowers.

In an instant, winter arrives.

Sculpted by fog
      A swan floats through
            A bed of silvery reeds

Bending seed tips
      This way and that.
            The world is not hidden.

Perfect equanimity:
      A mouthful of frost?
            A scattering of clouds?

Check!

So keen is our desire
      This patch-robed monk
            Spent decades

Piling snow
      Fine as rice powder
            Into an alabaster bowl.

LITANY ON THE BEACH
Gary Boelhower

Early morning on the warm beach,
a momentary Rosetta stone of glyphs
and runes, tracings of birds, mollusks,

and the moon's work, waits now
for the sea's erasure. The fisherman
is here again as sure as the sun's climb

out of the morning mist, already
dancing with his net and hungry eyes,
looking for lightning in the aqua water,

his fine mesh of dreams draped
over his arms and shoulders,
then flung out in a perfect circle.

In a fluid glissando his feet turn
in the white sand, his muscled arms
arc through the spume thrown up

by the surrendering waves.
Then he gathers it in, closes the circle,
pulls the net slowly to himself.

He seems to smile at the small fish
taken from this immensity of ocean,
then goes on dancing down the wide

aisles of the waking light, every
morning a litany of faith and longing.
Step now to the ocean's edge,

say your prayers into glinting luster,
throw your net, fling yourself
open toward the horizon.

BETWEEN US
Gary Boelhower

Sometimes the distance
        between us is light years,
                you in your dying, me

in my planning to keep
        the flowers watered and
                get the house painted

before the frost comes
        early in the fall. Death seeps
                into every syllable and finally

nothing is free of finitude,
        the counting of days,
                the names of the guardian angels.

But today you ask me to massage
        your feet and hands, so I sit
                on the edge of your hospital bed

and try to feel the marrow in your brittle
        bones, to soften the tendons taut as anchor
                lines in a harsh wind, to taste the ripe fruit

of now, to inhabit together the deepening
        silent sorrow. We have already entered
                that empty house of grief, you saying goodbye

to everything that touches your skin,
        me facing your banishment from
                this world, from your side of the bed.

CASTING OFF
Gary Boelhower

You will not give up
your body
reduced to sticks and a pulse
still you want to stay
in the house
of light
where the daisies
lift their plain and beautiful faces
and the poppies parade
their regal silks in the garden
outside your vigil
window
the yellow lilies
all you grew to love.

The cargo is unloaded
day by day almost invisible
the thick lines
are cast off
the heavy chain of reason
hauled up
with its anchor
of logic.

Still you want to walk
through the house
over and over
one small labored step
after another
looking at your legs
willing them to move
retracing steps
in all the streets
it was your pleasure to walk.

At last
a small round moan
rises from your marrow

and the dark entanglements of disease
a small round moan
with each breath
strains against the tide
that pulls you
at last
the silent sea.

APPEARANCES
Gary Boelhower

finding you in pieces
and places I can't expect
surprised by tablespoons
of tomato paste
you put in the freezer

books you've left a place marked
a clipping of Salisbury cathedral
stashed in the world atlas for our next trip

walking the Split Rock trail
your footsteps still echo

packing your shirts to give away
I repeat our ritual
button your collar
kiss your fresh shaved face

bowing to the yellow buds
in the rose garden
fragrance of all our anniversaries
your smile
in the folded silk of their petals

appearing in the orange of cantaloupes
smell of lemons
taste of caramel apples
anchovies
lamb chops

paying for Prosecco
at the liquor store
the man wonders at the tears
but doesn't ask

walking day after day
sad gratitude
like pebbles

36

in my shoes
unpredicted visits
your only touch

WEDDING PARTY
Greg Opstad

Six wildflowers,
dressed in springtime colors
blossom across the mountainside.
Who would have thought
such a bouquet could be so dazzling?
Lavenders, purples, pinks, and yellows
dance upon newfallen
snow. Each new flower,
straight and tall, lifts her face
to the sky and rivals the sun
with her simple joy.

BROKEN FISHING LINES
Greg Opstad

And my old fishing line driven upon the rocks
was what I thought about as we drove in hasty
silence back home. I'd snagged it on a branch
and broken both, but I was unable to get them back;
a ranger had just brought news of my grandfather
and there was still a six-hour drive. The black line
that spun off my reel was left to tangle with decaying
branches and fallen leaves washing the gray shoreline.
My fishing pole was tossed in a corner of the cabin
as my parents threw clothing and groceries in the car.
Soon my line, those branches, bits of leaves would be
fixed in November ice, but for a few more days
they would still splash against the rocks. For now
there was just the yellow wash of headlights aimed
away from the lake to Grand Marais, to Duluth
from Hinckley and Cambridge and at last, to Minneapolis
as the family begins to gather together in the cold night.

TARGET PRACTICE
Jan Chronister

Zinnia seeds fill my quiver
flat flakes of flint
tiny arrowheads with
pale petal shafts still attached.

I shoot them into furrows toward August
where they explode in fireworks
of gold and fuchsia.

I kneel to the power
of something so small and hard
magnets attracting moon messages
germinating
magically emerging in vibrant blooms.

As I plant
I feel a wound in my heart
as if some well-aimed ammunition
has found its mark.

FLOWERING

Jan Chronister

Fleeing Laos
she shouldered her husband's body
sown with shrapnel,
scooped up chemical coated river water.
At 52, planted in Wisconsin,
their bodies bloom with cancer.

In Hmong there is only the present,
no past or future perfect.
Mothers coax small children to school,
all with thick black tulip hair,
bundled against winter's cold
in a garden of bright hats and scarves.

SEVEN BRIDGES ROAD
Jane Barrick

Drive a straight, paved road
Sharp left onto gravel
Summertime smell: ragweed and army worm stench
Iron dust flying up, steep hill
No chance of scaling this in winter
A fork in the road brings you the choice between
Hawk Ridge and the Bridges
See for miles or look for tadpoles in the stream eddies
Marsh marigolds
The first bridge is most thrilling
Others bring a new joy — darker stone, arches,
Steep drop to the Lester River, rushing:
And water even through drought

Potholes made the driving rough, so Dad took the Jeep to town
No roof, no doors, my brother and I sat
On the wheel wells in back and bounced to Grandma and Grandpa's
Paul Harvey's voice over AM radio
Dewy mornings
Summer lay before us, the water warming,
Grandpa still young enough to drive us through town
To see the mansions old shipping money built:
Stone fortresses against a frigid lake
Looking back, I am glad this is what I remember. Know.
Spaghetti-strap sundresses and wildflowers in my hand
Not the emptiness of being away from her
Who would be away from him thereafter
Or the stream bed carved between them,
Over which we had already begun piling stones, mortar.

BLACKBURNIAN WARBLER
Janet Riegle

While the woods wait for daybreak,
a delicate warbler — back mostly black,
wings trimmed in white — zips to the
top of the tallest pine.

With beak pointed east,
he taunts the dawn
to outshine the orange
blaze of his breast.

TOWNSEND'S SOLITAIRE
Janet Riegle

They call you Solitaire, and how well you live up to your name.
We first met in December on a hazy zero day.
I was bundled up in fleece; you were huddled in a bare tree
with merely your feathers for shelter from those
frigid winds jingling the ice on Lake Superior.
But you had been beckoned by berries dangling
like Christmas lights from vines climbing an old stone wall.
After the train steamed past you careened across
the railroad tracks for a snack.

When the lake froze hard as marble I assumed you wouldn't stay.
But several days later I spotted you further down the tracks
jealously guarding the mountain ash and
buckthorn that clung to the steep cliff.
Days turned to weeks, then to months, and I wondered
why you had traveled hundreds of miles
to spend winter here in a deep freeze?
Maybe mountains asleep under fluffy blue fleece
forgot to provide for their feathered tenants.
Or do you — like other two-legged creatures —
prefer your fruit ice cold and fermented?

Spring brought fragrant breezes and it
seemed for a while they had swept you away,
until I heard a chattery tune and found you
perched on the spire of a spruce.
Your bubbly song sailed out on the lake.
Perhaps you were fishing for a feathered catch.

As spring progressed I guess you finally headed west
where cliffs stand taller and chances are greater
that you'll meet someone all dressed in feathers
the color of a cloudy dawn just as the sun
peers through the panes of her wings.

GO OUT
Janet Riegle

in homage to Robert Frost

In the hills near my home are some woods
where thrushes nest.
This evening I'll visit and hope
they will greet their guest.

When my feet leave the street for the path
all commotion fades,
just the sweep of a breeze through the leaves
where the woodcock wades.

As the wind settles down comes a melody
wild and sweet,
one that even the finest of flutists
could not repeat.

How vibrant the song as it spirals
round every tree.
Ornithology be damned — this Veery
sings only to me!

But no, I step too close and
he snaps his bill.
Now he's talking to me, saying
High-tail it down that hill!

THE NAKED THING
Jasmine Baumgart

My Dear Men,

Imagine. I am naked before you.
Breathe deep my bareness, the scent of
Sand. Warm, soft and never settled.
Stare. Do not blink. Come closer.
Drown in the brown of my hair.
Measure breaths by the rise of my chest,
Admire the curve and lift of my breast.
Think of me only as this — a body.
I am laid still and bare before you.

Before you begin to indulge your lust,
Look up. Look up! Look into my eyes.
This baring of skin is but a disguise,
Underneath is humanity filled with disgust
You see my body but look up. Look up!

I am a child you have seen sleeping
I am a secret you failed at keeping
I am a woman, raped and weeping

But I am not Adam's apple for eating.

I am the welcoming warmth of the wind before spring,
The finger freed from too tight a ring
The choked voice of Ophelia singing
The love-child of lesbians grinning
I am the breath of new life beginning.

Offering only what bare soul can bring
I am the beautiful, the naked thing.

MOTHER'S SCARVES
Jeanine Emmons

Women from many cultures have made use of the square head scarf, folded into a triangle, as head gear. In cold climates, the fabric was often wool. I think scarves are easier to wear than a hat. The term "babushka" is one term for this scarf and also means "grandmother" in Russian.

My mother wore a wool scarf on the farm where I grew up, and trained me to wear one also. I had a lot of ear infections in my preschool and early grade school years, and my mother tried to protect my ears from the cold. We did not use the term babushka, mom was Scandinavian. Somewhere along the line I heard the term, though, and knowing what it meant gave me a warm feeling.

Scarves did not catch on with my sister, ten years my junior. My mother and I had headscarves in common, and she passed some of hers on to me when I became an adult. It was a comfort to me to wear one of her scarves, I realize now. Once off the farm, my mother started wearing winter hats, or, if it was not very cold, light weight "see through" nylon scarves, or nothing on her head. She made a fine mink hat from a rummage sale find. She knitted a gold fluffy mohair hat which she wore for decades. She looked good in hats. I lived in the country and continued to wear headscarves well into my adulthood, although not to town. It was a habit for me. I had a yellow one, a black one and a plaid one, all passed to me by my mother.

Gradually I have let them go. I gave them to thrift stores, not being able to just throw them in the garbage. They were of good quality, fluffy woven wool, but I couldn't seem to find another use for them.

A few years ago I gave away my last wool headscarf. My winter headgear is now hats, most of which I have knitted myself.

My mother, now 89, still loves and cares for me. I treasure the memory of her tying a scarf under my chin, but I don't need to keep a babushka to recreate that good feeling.

ALTERED LANDSCAPES
Jeanne C. Maki

Mother watched as spruce began to sprout here and there in the hayfield and clumps of brush gain roothold along the ditches.

"Just look at that," she would say, angry, frowning. "Think of my father's years of hard work to clear those fields, how his back always hurt. And now your uncle is letting everything grow over."

She did have a point. I saw the spruce, the brush, the wildflowers replacing timothy, and I would mourn with her. Folks say it's a shame to see all the fields growing over, a shame that the work of those who cleared the land cannot be honored by keeping the land cleared.

But yet this shallow clay over granite at the tip of the watershed in northern Minnesota was never fertile farmland. Seventy-five, a hundred years ago a family could survive up here with a couple milk cows and a vegetable garden and firewood and blueberries up on the hill. Today most folks think this way of life is an anachronism.

On one of Uncle's visits from the nursing home back to the farm, he and I stood in the yard looking across the creek to the back fields. The creek had been sand-bottomed when he and Mother were young, before the banks were logged for fields. By my childhood, fragile topsoil had covered the sand with thick silt. Twenty years ago the beavers took over, and the creek now winds through a wetland of marsh grass.

For a while we were silent, listening to the ducks. Then I broached the subject. "Spruce starting to come up over there," I said, pointing. "Yah," he said, thoughtfully. "It's just the natural evolution of the landscape."

The natural evolution of the landscape. No anger, no guilt, no regret. Just acceptance, serenity, expectation.

DRIVING
Jennifer Derrick

I am in the car
when I think of you
realizing with sudden lucidity
that we live our lives in
each other's absence.

SISTER
Jennifer Derrick

I am glad to see you here
graceful and supple
strong back muscles
holding up the weight of your womb.

There, in that soft galaxy
dark, liquid, calm
new life grows each day.
A little star suspended.

You move slower now
content to rest
lounging on pillows
laughing late into the night
in bed beside me.

THE HENHOUSE
Jennifer Derrick

I walk in timidly
stepping carefully
amidst roosts and poop
feed and heat lamps
rustling and clucking hens.

A speckled brown egg
freshly laid
cracks as I pick it up
warm hands are fire
on this ice-cold morning.

Standing here,
I remember the country in me
skinned knees filled with
bronzed Alabama dirt;
fried okra, butchering time
that six-year-old farm girl
cradling chicks and eggs
in her tanned, chapped hands.

INTERRUPTED
Jill Hinners

At the stove squatting in its old cramped corner,
I stirred my sauce with a thick wooden spoon
neither saving the world nor even coming close.

The radio sang "Settled Down Like Rain," and then,
we interrupt this broadcast to report that the plane
bearing Senator Wellstone has disappeared in flight.

I waited, stirring slowed. My heart crept into my ears
and I cocked my head to hear above the din.
Indeed, the plane was missing, communication lost.

My stirring speeded up. Around and around
went my hand, the spoon, the sauce;
they circled, an orbit around the unthinkable.

How many revolutions did they make before the worst:
the plane had crashed; all passengers likely gone.
Once again, he is in the room with me,

at the head of the class, his syllabus a call to act,
his wrestler's body erupting with his words, and today,
one last fiery explosion of that voice had burst

from its compact source as flames, shooting up up
out of the swampy thicket, out of the Iron Range,
out of the wreckage — passion illuminating slate gray sky

before burning itself completely out.
A lone spark fell; who would catch its light?
My spoon dropped from my grasp or rather, I unclasped it,

let the handle tip against the side of the pot,
half submerged. I studied the lines on my empty palm
as if I could find there something else to hold.

ENTER THIS MOMENT
Jim Perlman

for M.M.

Enter this moment, south Minneapolis, circa 1960. Father
hauls out a leather case stamped POLAROID from the front
hall closet that smells of Revelation pipe tobacco and fur-
trimmed winter coats. Perhaps it's mid-December and mother
has already hung her nylons as Christmas stockings, filled
with apples and oranges.

You and I poised atop the lime green living room sofa when
the flash erupts. We're happily neighborhood friends, our ten-
year-old boy selves mimic each other like cupped hands.
Your head leans towards me. Soon enough, I'd wear eye
glasses because you had them first.

I can't remember — did we cut our right palms to bleed then
and become blood brothers with a handshake?

Fifty years later and this image stares out of the memory fog,
printed on paper thin as a Communion wafer.

The fathers have all since died — yours, mine, Bud Conrad,
Mr. Cousins, Fred Opie Sr.

Our family home purchased by the Fayhees, leveled, then
rebuilt.

A few elm trees gone from disease and high winds.

No one who lived here can ever come back again.

HE SAYS, I SAY
Jody J. Bassett

When he says "I'm sorry," I say "Whatever."

When he says "I love you," I say "You don't know what love is."

When he says "I promise," I say "For the 100th time..."

When he says "I'll give you all the money," I say "Oh brother."

When he says "Come back," I say, "I've given 13 years."

When he says "Let's start over," I say, "Show me AA tokens."

When he says "I've changed," I say, "I'm happy for you."

When he says, "Call me," I don't answer the phone!

TONIGHT
John McCormick

tonight
it should be a prayer
that age old
descriptor
of longing and beauty
Oh Creator
Oh Spirit
we have come together
tonight
it should be a prayer
that ends in resolve
to be changed
to be change
to give thanks
to our selves
for each other
tonight
it should be a prayer
with endless prepositions
in name
by grace
through the needle's eye
onto judgment
until
tonight
it should be a prayer
of reflection
reaction
reduction
revolution
revelation
rejoice
resolve
tonight

it will be prayer

TWO DAYS
Julie Brooks Barbour

Two days after my daughter's birth, jaundice sets in.
Doctor's orders: sunbathe or else phototherapy.
Two days after my daughter's birth, the sun beams into the apartment
like a beacon and I assume the task of moving my girl towards health.
Three decades old, its right arm wobbly, the rocking chair creaks
back and forth as we sway in a square of warm light.
A cap tops my daughter's head. Blankets that surround her
I open toward the sun, wrinkled arms and legs now bare.
Her dark eyes slowly close. I do not think beyond this moment.
I do not think at all. We rock and the day moves forward.

TELEPHONE WIRE
Julie Gard

I stood in Akhmatova's kitchen. Clothes hung drying and made the room damp, said the brochure. People wandered through like in any communal apartment and whispered into the phone. She walked among them in genteel slippers, halfway to the afterlife.

There is nothing to say that Blok has not said, Mandelstam, Brodsky, Altman, Modigliani. Tsvetaeva shaped her name into an old and slow lament.

She chose to stay with her people. I sat next to her on a wooden chair, ignoring the rope and sign. Our mouths were smoky with cigarette and potato. We waited for the afternoon mail and the fall of the most recent empire, for some word of what had happened and what was to come.

WHEN THE MIND IS READY
Karen Keenan

1.
It started as only a fleeting comment upon the death of parents.
A fact revealed from one friend to another.

"Those old family pictures in the attic, most likely of relatives — since we
can't identify anyone, my sister and I threw them into the trash."

2.
Years later, feet step over the Bedford Avenue threshold of a Williamsburg
junk shop neatly arranged with attractive secondhand household items.
Eyes fix on a boot box full of discarded black and white photos.

Fingers touch images bordered in saw-tooth edged frames.
One calls for closer inspection.

Four adults stand on grass in front of a white clapboard barn, three males
and one female. She wears a flower print dress, the men in farmer's clothing
— well worn. Siblings perhaps? It must be a happy day. Broad smiles grace
four faces.

Lifetimes are fleeting.
Family work is calling.

3.
A cold March morning sun beckons New York tourists to gather warmth
from a corner building's bright red brick wall.

Listen.

One voice rises above the Brooklyn Heights busy intersection.
With head tightly protected by a green and blue scarf, a softly aged woman
chats on a cell phone, stops, looks for the streetlight to change.

She says, "I love you.
Honey, you just gotta stop thinking and start doing."

Streetlight turns green, chatter fades into the day. Her directive lingers.

4.

Back in Duluth with morning coffee and the Sunday newspaper, a familiar routine returns. First read the national news, then the local, followed by the comics and want ads.

Eyes catch something interesting in the community education section — a course on how to work with family archives.

Like a teenager receiving a new school year class list, a mind eagerly anticipates the appearance of a new teacher.

TENDER INSIGHTS
Karen Keenan

You, dear daughter, call it clutter.
Too much stuff here and there with no thought of beauty.
What? Really?

> Yes.
> Now let's do something about it.
> Take stuff from the shelf, the cupboards, drawers and cubbies.
> Sort it.
>
> That handmade oval woven straw box with a lid: do you need it?
> Why?
>
> You don't?
> OK, trash or donation? These are some choices.

Oh, this is not fun. I'd rather pass.

> No.
> Let's do this for a short time.
> Only an hour.
> You'll feel so much better.
> It will look good in here. Now it makes me anxious.

OK, no I don't need that — or that.
Well...
That hand size pink polka-dotted plastic horse reminds me of you as a
small child.

You, dear son, simply say there is too much paper in this house.
Books, magazines, music.
Pictures, letters, notebooks.
You live upstairs and store stuff downstairs in our old bedrooms.

I see.
Cherish, release, accept, evolve.
Really.

DUET
Kat Mandeville

Beneath chiffon sleeves her forearms are massive
with years spent holding up collapsible worlds, her mind
a sandcastle, her eyes washing up like milk glass.

Today, her arms particularly tired, she pins herself under
the strings of her Steinway. *I can survive any melody*
she whispers, *Even my own.* And lies

there all afternoon, the pressure cracking
two ribs, her varicose ankles soft on the wooden
black-lacquered lip and the piano

born in London, bullied in Berlin,
warped in New York, now resting in Waco

finally given its chance to show her mercy
closes on her
and swallows.

SKIPPING TO MIDDLE CHAPTERS FOR GRAPHIC DESCRIPTION
Kat Mandeville

was the night Pittsburgh flooded
with the sky, our dark neighborhood
sewn crisscross, a crucifix of rain.

Topless, I entered the storm
as lightning, as Cassandra making Apollo
thrust for dawn. And you,

a porch-dweller, stayed behind
and watched, sucked a cigarette
mumbling, *God only loves you*

for your tits, and they're boring anyway,
then came all over the perennials
lining the yard.

*

until grade school years later. I sucked
fireball jawbreakers, my precious jewels
while hanging upside-down on monkey bars.

The boy I hadn't noticed said,
Only one thing you should choke on,
poked in, pulled out the steaming

ruby, poised it on his fingers like a jeweler
winking back. Forgetting me, he slimed it on his
lips, cracked it on his teeth and swallowed

*

when Grandmother kissed
my four-year-old mouth, whispered into it
Regard hope with little hands.

Smell like a good fight. Beware the creature
who takes the god out of you — your night-sugar.
Fills your body with his salt. These thieves,

the best of them will find you.
I asked what of the ones wanting respect?
In my ear she laughed. Barely.

Go. Give their tiny minds
what you do not need.
The rest is yours.

We'll welcome you back to the homeland
when all his seed is spent on stony ground.
Bra in your back pocket. His teeth in your mouth.

AN EARLY LESSON IN GRIEF
Kathleen McQuillan

My paternal grandparents Vern and Hortense McQuillan lived in a well-kept middle class neighborhood on Detroit's East Side in a town called St. Clair Shores. Their single story brick home was surrounded by mature elm and oak trees and was situated on a paved street with curbs, a long drive from my parents' little two-bedroom bungalow on Detroit's west side in an area on the edge of cornfields, far enough out of town to still be on gravel with ponds full of pollywogs and ditches perfect for play. Because of the distance, our family only went there on holidays, and every Easter in particular I got to stay for a whole week with my grandparents all by myself.

My grandfather always wore white shirts and creased grey trousers with a belt that encircled his rather generous midriff. He was a tall, squarely built man with thick silver grey hair through which he would run his large fingers, an idiosyncratic gesture along with the special way he fanned his large hand across his forehead when he would sit in his favorite chair and tell stories. When Grandpa was present, all attention was on him as he spun a tale, punctuated by his dry wit and pointed criticisms, most often directed at Grandma and if not at her, then at Republicans.

Grandma was immaculate in her personal appearance. Every hair was in place. Her short sleeved shirtwaist dress perfectly pressed. She always wore nylon stockings and high heeled shoes, even when she was cleaning the house. She never learned to drive and so her place was squarely "in the home," keeping the house as immaculate as she kept herself. A hankie was always tucked neatly in her sleeve. The house felt big to me, with its sparse but smart furnishings, and its big (and seldom entered) basement.

I remember Grandma's kitchen cabinets filled with interesting appliances, things my mother did not have, including an electric frying pan, a multispeed mixer with its set of multi-sized stacking bowls, and a deep fry donut maker. Grandma made the best donuts I had ever eaten. There was a huge drop-leaf table in the dining room, the perfect place under which to hide my small pre-school body at times when the need for solitary refuge — even in my early childhood — would overwhelm me. Grandma was a quiet woman who went about her routine, dusting her prized possessions, running her monstrous vacuum cleaner, barely taking notice of me. I had learned early on "to be seen and not heard." It was with Grandma and

Grandpa Mac that I was sent to stay when my cancer ridden father slipped toward the final days of his life.

My daddy had returned from one of his many trips to the hospital, a little more misshapen and grotesque, from my young child's viewpoint. A strange-looking bed was placed in my and my sister's bedroom. This is where he would stay now, my mother explained, and we would sleep on the couch. His skin was dark yellow, his eyes lifeless. I was kind of afraid to look at his bony body all curled up in his bed. He barely looked at me. He smelled funny and made strange sounds when he breathed.

On my dresser at the head of his bed, was a small altar with a statue of the Blessed Mother standing in her bare feet on a hand crocheted snow white doily. I remember her serene gaze, her open hands, her long white veil and her beautiful sky blue dress with a circle of tiny gilded stars surrounding her heart. My big sister always kept a small dark blue vase filled with flowers there, sometimes lilacs or lilies of the valley, picked from my mother's well-tended beds.

As a small child, I always had a penchant for "running away." I kept a small plaid metal skatecase under my bed with a favorite outfit and a few special things inside. Late in August, 1959, my mother told me to pack my suitcase while she packed another with an assortment of clothing and my tooth-brush. I did what I was told. I left one afternoon with my grandparents. No explanations were given. We took the long drive, I and my grandparents, across the big city of Detroit. My grandmother led me to the room where I would sleep. She took my clothes and placed them in a big drawer in a big, big dresser.

On the next page of my memory, the room where my grandparents slept appears. There is their huge imposing bed, a long low dresser with a mirror that reached almost to the ceiling, and an assortment of hand-cut glass containers filled with very shiny copper pennies. Grandpa's ties were draped neatly over the frame of the mirror as if that was where they truly belonged. The shades were always drawn.

Each morning I helped Grandma make her bed — I on one side, she on the other. We pulled the white chenille spread up and over a pair of voluptuous pillows, stationed side by side where the two had lay their heads the night before. Grandma made sure we were in perfect unison as the bed-making was completed. And then the words came out. "Your daddy died last night."

I don't remember saying a word. But there must have been a look. The next thing I remember was my grandmother admonishing in a low, firm voice, "And you must be a little soldier and not cause your mother a bit of trouble."

That became the 11th Commandment, "Thou shalt not cause your mother a bit of trouble." This would be my first and only lesson about loss. I later learned that my grandmother was an expert on grief. My father was her third child to die.

For a little girl just six years old, I guess Grandma thought this simple statement would cover a big, complicated topic. My father's death was never mentioned again.

MY MOTHER BAKES CAKES
Kim Sisto-Robinson

> *We will drink red wine together and remember leaning back to back against each other — laughing, dreaming of being beautiful old ladies charming gray-haired men — Marian Aitches*

Everybody has been coping with my sister's murder in different ways.

Me? I wail, scream, lament, and moan like a wounded dog. I awaken in the middle of the night to moonless skies and dark waters. I dream fragmented dreams that terrify me.

I asked my sister in one of these nightmares, "What the hell happened?" And she responded, "He shot me three times."

I despise the murderer, but I don't spend my time hating.

Generally, I spend my days and nights drenched in tears; so many tears. I spend my moments trying to find God again. I spend my minutes thinking about what my sister's future might have been. I contemplate how I will move forward without splattering all over the floor again and again and again.

And I get aggravated effortlessly.

Yesterday, somebody stated stupidly, "Oh, my knees hurt." I spurted back at them, "I don't give a shit. My sister is dead."

I'm not enjoyable to be around these days. The man we ate Sunday dinners with killed my sister. Did you expect me to stroll around talking about the fucking weather or your idiotic sore knees?

At any rate...

My brother copes by working out. He sweats. He pumps iron. He goes to the spa to set the treadmill on fire. His smile is not the same. When I look inside his eyes, I see the pain, the loss, the absurdity of it all. I see my sister's face. I see myself.

My dad lifts weights, too. Sometimes he sits on the oak swing in his back garden staring into space. He plays golf with my sister's boys. He wraps his arms around me and says he loves me more than usual. When I look into his sweet, dark face, I see a 70 year old man who has lost his daughter. I see the child he once was. I see myself.

Lost.   Looking.   Longing.

My mother washes clothes, waxes floors, vacuums carpets, cleans windows, but mostly, she bakes cakes. She uses buttermilk in all of her recipes: chocolate coffee cake topped with old-fashioned cocoa frosting, rhubarb cinnamon cake, banana cake smothered with Philadelphia cream cheese icing.

She is a Goddess. She is our Mother Theresa. She is the Glue-God that keeps the family moving forward, onward, functioning.

"Sweetheart, did you know that I can make four cakes from a half gallon of buttermilk?" she says.

When I walk into my mother's house on Seaver Avenue, the scent of chocolate fills the air, cinnamon lingers, sugar and cocoa simmer and bubble on her twenty year old stove.

It all appears so normal. So utterly ordinary. Unchanged.

I almost expect my sister to be sitting at the kitchen table with that pink-lipsticked grin on her face playfully teasing, "Hey, Kimmy, split a piece of mom's low fat cake with me, will ya?"

But she is gone. Gone. Three gunshots. Then gone.

I am gone.

What remains is an empty chair, a flower left out, and a void so massive that I gasp at the size of it.

When I think about the horrific change in our family, sometimes I can't catch my breath. I am forced to fall to my knees. I am forced to cry out to my silent God.

I look at my mother's appearance as she serves me a piece of chocolate cake; her bottom lip begins to tremble, her brown eyes fill up with moisture, her mascara begins to run.

She squeezes my hand and whispers, "Honey, I have a little buttermilk left, I think I'll make a cinnamon rhubarb cake tomorrow."

THE CAGED BIRD DOES NOT SING
Kim Sisto-Robinson

> *The free bird leaps on the back of the wind and floats downstream till the current ends and dips his wings in the orange sun rays and dares to claim the sky* — Maya Angelou

"I know what's different about you," I said to my sister on our last walk.

"What?" She smiled.

"You don't need me like you used to. I like that. I like that you're finally coming into your own skin. It's about time, Sis. When do you sign the divorce papers?"

"In a couple weeks." She grasped my hand tightly.

"LIBERATION!" She squealed. "I can't wait to get away from that man, get my own house, begin a fresh life."

My sister never got the chance to sign those divorce papers. Her soon to be ex-husband killed her two days after that walk.

We were going to have a surprise shower for her. An "Emancipation Shower." A "New Beginnings Shower." Candles & Cosmopolitans. Salsa & Sangria. Sushi & Sex and The City.

We were going to fill her new home with love, love, love.

We talked about painting her living room some funky color like bubblegum pink or crazy cranberry. We talked about how nice it was to see her smile again.

He left work early on May 26th. He sat on the couch like a demon-devil and waited and waited. He was never a man, so I shall call him "the murderer" or "the devil."

Nevertheless, he was not what she deserved, or for that matter, what the world deserved.

He was nothing at all.

The Beretta pistol was so small, the devil could conceal inside the palm of his sweaty hand. I imagine he rubbed the iron between his fingers anticipating her absence, his absence, his final control. I imagine he tasted the metal upon his toxic tongue. I presume he was prepared to go straight to HELL.

She came home from work about 5:00, ran upstairs to put on her walking clothes and hoisted her hair in a ponytail. She texted our dad.

"I'll see you on the trail, Pop. I love you."

Her last words. The last time she'd walk down the steps. Her final beautiful breaths.

   And mine.

He locked the front door, lingered like a predator.

Perhaps he said a prayer to whomever murderers utter prayers. Perhaps he gave last rites to himself.

I wonder why God didn't intervene. Why He'd allow the cage to remain closed.

There were two alternatives. She stayed with him or she died with him.

He placed the gun to the back of her beautiful head, her healthy head. He blasted three times to make sure. He had to make damn sure my sister never gained consciousness, had to make damn certain she couldn't fly away.

Maya Angelou was wrong when she said the caged bird sings. That's just not true. The caged bird cannot sing until she is set free; she cannot form a pleasing melody of verse until the cage is swung wide open. Only then will she sing her sweet song of freedom. Only then will her wings reach the orange of the sun's rays.

Sing, My Sweet Sister.
   Sing. Sing. Sing.

RISING
Kyle Elden

Don't give your life away to sorrow
to watch its flames take everything into
burning light, to watch the smoke
of your dreams spell out the language
of longing and loss, to hang heavy in your clothes
and on your hair forever

When you arrive at this place
and find yourself covered in the mud
in this thickness you walk through
get down on your knees, prayer on your breath
dirt on your lips — and like the lotus flower
submerged in swamp, rise laughing
and red, bright as Jupiter pulling
her many moons in a tidal dance

DOORWAY
Kyle Elden

Your palm glides across
a door
the smell of wood and old paint
presses against the last thing
between you
and the life
that awaits

Your fingers clasp
cold brass doorknob
and turn, open
light begins to filter in
and you know
it is time

You have learned what can be learned
here

You cannot look back
cannot stay
the past becomes the past
and you do the only thing you can do

Words like
regret and
if only
fall away like feathers
from a bird in flight
softly floating downward
white
against blue sky

BECOMING TEA
Kyle Elden

It is only red mug
with hot water, and
a tea bag steeping
releasing golden brown
steam rising
with light
with the easy scent of peppermint
a ritual of lips to cup, and
warmth flows gently
falling down throat
into belly

An act of surrender
so simple
held by a single thread
delicate dark leaf
inside the boundary of tea bag
infused with what is
to transform into something
different
something more
unlocked,
released

LEAVING
Kyle Elden

When people leave us
they are never really gone.

When in thick folds of sleep
you come back
I see your face, of which I know
every soft edge
your head presses against my shoulder
my hands run through your hair
fingers familiar with your texture,
curve of scalp
your lips turn gently to smile
we laugh
bellies rise and fall
because here,
we have not yet lost
one another.

When you come back in
Fleet Foxes debut album
blasting through my car's speakers,
coffee brewing and scrambled eggs with
spinach, tomatoes, and polenta,
the night sky hung with stars and
snow fall cold, melting against skin
trekking across frozen river on snowshoe,
smell of red curry lentil soup and
warm bread with butter.

When you come back,
you are the dark oiled mark of a fingerprint,
love forever in my blood
in my thoughts when all else is quiet
no one is around, the distance could not
be greater but you are near
you never fully left
your spirit touched mine
rearranged, reconstructed, chipped away

helped form who I am today.

When you come back,
I am not a ghost town
vacant, broken down, void of life
I am a museum of flesh touched
and touching one another
floor boards worn differently because
of the way you walked across to greet me,
to hold me, to love me, and to hurt me
even if just in the leaving
and in the way you always stay.

MAMA FROG GOES BACK TO WORK
Laura Krueger-Kochmann

"It must be nice to have an adult conversation again,"
they say,
full of themselves
and little else.
Beneath their smiling veneer
a crumbling structure,
lonely dust
and rocks always shifting underfoot.
I am amphibian
drifting between two worlds.
Remembering the water, the light

glimmering movement
living and pure,
I yearn for the liquid language
of touch,
the smell of small kisses,
a closeness that is unconfined.

THE PRUNING
Leah Rogne

Listing badly, my father walked into the room carrying a small branch. He'd taken his walker and gone out for an early morning walk along the planting just across the driveway at the farm. It was a warm June day, but he had bundled up in a heavy coat and a hat with earlaps. He wouldn't wear his new prosthetic shoes, so he lumbered uncertainly as he shuffled along.

"I don't know what this is," he said.

"It's a honeysuckle," I said.

"How do you know?"

"Because you told me so," I said.

He looked at the branch dubiously, turning it over and over. "But honey-suckle is a vine," he said.

"Well," I said, "In some parts of the country it's a vine. But here it's a bush. It's got those rounded leaves and, see here, the little pinkish flowers with a bit of yellow inside? It grows east of the barn and in the tree rows south of the buildings where you planted them."

Frowning in disbelief, he continued to twirl the branch and stare at it as though I was lying, as though he'd never seen anything like it before. And, to him, he hadn't.

All my being rebelled at his disordered thinking. Anger rose in my throat as I continued to harangue him with information about the nature of the stem, the leaves, and flowers, data that would inevitably result in his real-ization of the identity of this plant. Try as I might, I couldn't convince him that he knew what a honeysuckle was and that this item fit into the honey-suckle category. This was a man to whom grasses, shrubs, trees, weeds, and every growing thing had been his life's work and the center of his passion. He knew, I knew, everything about plants. He could name every leafy thing and tell me why it was, what it was, what it wasn't, and why. Now, grizzled and unshaven, thin and shaky, puzzled and defiant, he sat there brooding and silent.

I loved my father. But like Dylan Thomas, I was raging, raging against the dying of the light in my father's mind. If he were one of my clients, I would have said something like, "Did you enjoy working with plants?" "How did you learn to identify plants?" "What kind of plants did you have on the farm?" "What's the right time to prune a shrub — is it better to do it in the fall or the spring?" "What difference does it make?" "How does pruning affect the flowers the next spring?" I'd try to redirect his emotion away from the cognitive deficit, try to build on his relationship to plants, help him find a pathway to his remaining mental strengths.

Instead, I felt like slapping him or shaking him into submission to my reality. For every error, for every mistake, for every muddled gaze he made toward the things that used to drive his life, his essence was fading, and I wanted him back. This is not somebody else's father, whom I would treat with endless patience and tenderness. This was MY father, and he was disappearing before my eyes.

This frail man sitting dazed in the chair was not my father; my father was a handsome, dark skinned young farmer who smelled of sweat, straw, and axle grease. My father had a spring in his step. He never walked when he could run, climbed down from a hayrack when he could jump, or went to church when he could work in the field. He knew everything.

But whether it was a honeysuckle or some exotic species as yet unknown to man and nature, it needed watering. So, my father limped outside to set up the hose to water the plants. In the struggle with the hose, he fell down. Ten days later he died of a bleed in his brain.

The day after he fell, his brain, bathed in fresh blood, seemed to re-fire and re-focus. He told me how he wanted me to help him get the garden in order because he and my mother couldn't take care of all of it any longer. He listed the flowers — by name — that he wanted to keep and those he wanted to abandon. He was alert, strong, handsome. I think he smelled just a bit of sweat, straw, and axle grease, even though the wheat harvest was months ahead — indeed, years behind.

The next day the clotting blood began to take its toll, and he quickly shrank into yet another world, losing his ability to walk, talk, eat, and eventually to breathe. On the ninth day, as my family kept vigil, I trimmed the dogwood just outside the front door. I came in and told him that I'd pruned the dogwood and I thought he'd be pleased. He died within the hour.

I took the dogwood cuttings and laid them in a wreath around his bed. When the funeral home came to get his body, they set the branches on the windowsill. I know they're dogwood because my father told me. I don't know if I pruned it right, because my father couldn't tell me. I know I pruned it at the wrong time for next year's flowers, but it was the right time for my father and me. For better or for worse, it will flower by the door each year from now on, and that may, some day, be enough.

THE BEANBAG
Linda LeGarde Grover

When the snow began to thaw, at first we saw
only a trace of flowered calico,
then every day more cotton flowers bloomed,
budding blue flowers wet with melting snow.
Familiar, it looked. I remembered
forget-me-nots on an old woman's house dress
that, when worn out and discarded she crocheted
into a rug, mostly; the smallest scrap
she sewed into a child's toy, a beanbag.

I remember that dress.
As a child, when she held me close to her,
my head against her soft, flowered middle,
smelling starch and warm geranium
in her soft and cool fleshy embrace
I felt brave, looking out at the world
from that bastion of blue flowered cloth.

Early in spring, after she died,
one day I recognized that flowered dress,
forget-me-nots on cotton, wet buds of blue flowers
on a beanbag we were kicking around the yard.

Split, it spilled the past

> her kitchen floor,
> bumpy patterned linoleum, shiny and bare
> reflecting wavy geraniums in coffee cans

nurtured from seeds of their own great-grandmothers

> checked oilcloth
> leaned to white pearl scallops at the edge
> by her daughters' slender, bending waists

and ground to silver dollars, several pairs,
by her ravenous sons' elbows

kitchen woodstove a hot dull black
bread baking in the oven
while above, noodles boil and tomatoes roil
singing huffs of steam above our heads

I remembered, when the beanbag spilled the past;
when it split and spilled the past, I remembered
and picked it up, to see it one more time

and what was that? I looked close, and closer.
Through its fraying, of returning to the earth,
the bag held life beyond the tiny past.
Split and spilt, its damp side finely pierced
by a infant bean seedling yet blind, but greedy
for the light, born in a cocoon of flowered
blue calico, a pattern wet with snow
forget-me-nots an early sign of spring
entwined now with a trace of tender green.

That dress; I remember her flowered dress.

PARTURITION, A POEM FOR BRENDA
Linda LeGarde Grover

Having won the game of patience seven times
and lost four I re-rubberband the deck.
my legs writhe restlessly, straighten I rise
to stand on dusty gray linoleum,
soles balance my weight, my soul my wait
      which excites the labor room nurse
      "Look how limber she is! Jumped right off that bed!
      Good idea, walk...walk...that'll get that baby out.
      Ring if you need me!" from a great distance it seems
      she bubbles through waves, and waves
thus grounded perhaps in control of my destiny,
the sullen indignities of these hours cumbrous
on my unseen feet, yellow with cold I imagine
that walk a crescent fertile and horseshoe-shaped
around the bed and back, around and back;
above, my yet unbirthed motherspirit
listens to seasounds from the swimmer within.

      After countless paced crescents she startles me,
an old woman with lined elm bark face and calm eyes
watching me through a small window in the wall
      "Grandmother? " I wonder, heartened
      by this visit I have wished for in my dreams
      since the day she died two months
      into my own conception
then realize the window is a mirror, and I an ageless crone at twenty-two.

      In that dimension past where numbers end
but not this walk and wait, yoked to this time
and clutching to each hip a fist of cloth,
blue fleur-de-lis on a tattered hospital gown
barefoot left crescent turn right crescent turn
as the waves crest, break, recede   crest, break recede

it stops, silences. *Where are the seasounds?*

      I have worn a shining silver omega
that frames the bed, gray linoleum shined

and buffed by my blessedly pain-free feet
that now step cautiously past my cronehood
and syncopate dustily toward my husband,
who sleeps in a harvest gold vinyl chair with chrome legs
> *"Can you hear that?" I inhale to form the words*
> *"I can't hear the seasounds anymore."*
but in that breath the swimmer turns, the silence breaks
with a pop as water rushes, flooding my cold yellow feet
with warm waves that carry dust bunnies
from beneath the bed to the corners of the room
out the door and down the corridor
to the nurse's station.
I complete my inhalation. Should I ring?
> *"Did you hear something?" my husband asks*
> *through the pitch of the rippling sea*
> *"Did you hear something?" he asks the girl I used to be.*

BLENDER ENVY
Linda M. Johnson

The bridal shower was held Friday night
before Minnesota's deer opener.
The shower planners timed it right;
hunting widows packed the place.
I was squished with cousins in the back
of the local community hall.
When the bride-to-be opened gifts,
they used our table for their display.
Sumptuous towels, high-thread-count sheets.
Flatware service for eight, fine china.
Colorful everyday pottery, canisters.
Baking pans, mixing bowls, measuring cups.
Gleaming stemware, wine rack, a bottle of merlot.
Two cookbooks, wooden spoons, a Crockpot.
It was fun to watch until she opened the final gift,
a shiny stainless steel blender with glass carafe.
I realized I was jealous; I wanted new stuff.
I wanted to be a young bride again,
anxious for our rose-tinted future,
where a matching set of dreams waited for us,
ready to be unwrapped.
At home that night I looked around.
I noticed silverware from several sets,
mismatched coffee cups, flannel sheets.
We didn't have fine china, could use new towels.
I also realized I wasn't envious anymore,
even though the blender went kaput.
I recognized we had a comfortable marriage,
a little worn from years gone by but it ran well
despite wrong buttons we'd pushed along the way.
It wasn't shiny and new but that was okay.
Instead I had the patina of facial lines, silver hair
on the man who could still make me laugh out loud.
I got undressed, climbed into bed.
Even after many years a matching set of dreams
waited for us, ready to be unwrapped.
We held each other through the night,
and didn't have to write thank you notes
in the morning.

THE MESSENGERS
Lisa Poje Angelos

One day the sign of transformation came
it floated in on monarch wings
in August of that year we lost you
we didn't take the hint
didn't know what we were seeing
we simply marveled
at this once in a lifetime visit
for days the driveway came to motion
the neighbor's flowered fields aloft
a soft fluttering of orange and black
I walked for the mail as if in a dream
clouds of the butterflies activating from
their perches swirling ahead of me
and again alighting in the dappled sun
there were hundreds, no thousands
I'd seen pictures of the clusters hanging
from the trees in Mexico
never imagined them here in the North
but each night at dusk in a mystically
coordinated ballet they gathered on the birches
bodies linked in hanging chains and as if by
a master switch in one fraction of a second
every single flutter stopped motionless
in another of nature's beautiful illusions
each wing took the apparent form of a leaf
and in the dim illumination one could not
have said if there were butterflies or
simply leaves and shadows
their delicate fragility so profound
their journey ahead so long and perilous
when finally full of nectar and rested
ready for the flight along Lake Superior
they disappeared as suddenly as they had come
we hadn't heard what they were telling
egg, caterpillar, chrysalis, butterfly and then?
the cyclic epitome of life energy changing forms
it wasn't a week that they were gone
before the phone call came

UNBIDDEN
Lisa Poje Angelos

There are those rare days
when breath catches in the throat
at the sight of something unbidden
but just exactly needed
tiny green eggs in a nest delicately
nestled amongst soft moss
a frond of fern tightly wound
like a child's hand around an adult finger
reminding of the promises of life
the small beginnings and
the path of dramatic unfolding
the moment of actually seeing
your grandmother again
in the small girl's mischievous
glance, the form of her hands
something imagined somewhere
in the deep folds of the mind
something indeterminately hoped
for dares to appear catching us
off guard demanding a happy
smile we thought we had
long lost the ability to muster

TONIGHT
Liz Minette

Tonight the snowy back yard
is a landscape of light.

So much that the party
of animal tracks — rabbit,
squirrel, bird, human, —
are clearly visible,
a small cosmic map
of our survival and curiosity:

shelter under cedar;
a tussle near the Colorado pine;
skittering along the treeline;
boot prints to investigate
these other wanderings.

One red feather on top of the snow.

Even the neighbor's cat's
nightly visits are betrayed
by the ghost of her velvet feet,
strung like pearl steps,
single file and straight up
the middle of the driveway.

Right now, the clock beats
toward midnight. And the house
is cold as another full moon
slowly circles again, home
to its own traces and signs.
Its rhythm, like everything,
showing us where we've been,
where we're going.

ONE
Liz Minette

One stone, picked
from the sand
on a walk along
Wisconsin Point.

That summer day,
hot, like a dream
from long ago,
I didn't ask
the stone if it
wanted to leave.

The person I walked with
and the person I was
long gone, changed.
Yet we still know
each other.

Oil from my fingers
over the years
has left a dark smudge,
my trace on its
resting side.

And its own markings:
fine, elliptic circles
on its face, like
spider's thread,
a delicate labyrinth,
that is crossed
again and now with
small grey flecks,
constellations,
a galaxy of windows
and doors, maybe,
to let in music.

Or perhaps more

to hold a stone's secrets,
its dreams —

its memory of water
and being in another place
once.

AT SOLSTICE
Liz Minette

A full moon flags
the December barn.

There is only this light
on the way to evening chores.

Two horses softly walk
to the fence, stand
shoulders rounded
smooth as planets.

Both are curious for anything
my hands hold: a touch,
apple slices, the heat of oats.

Zoie the farm dog has come along with me.
She wouldn't have it any other way.

Inside the barn, two cats,
buddhas on a ledge, intently watch
Zoie's barrel shaped body
scuttle after one scent to another.

Hens thump to their roost
under the heat lamp and
their movements sound
like boxes falling.

I exchange new straw
for coops' small harvest —
three eggs tonight.

Cracking two over the cats' feed,
I place the third in my coat
and then Zoie and I walk
the long driveway.

The moon follows, casts

shadow among birch, and
in front of us, as dog and human
try to catch up to themselves.

Back to the house's soft watch,
Zoie's last two puppies, Jasmine, Kebu,
spring from the kennel when I open it.

They greet us jumping, crushing
the egg I've forgotten —

small return of sun in my pocket.

HONOR
Loree Miltich

At the place where, unmarked, two roads cross
we lost two sisters traveling
to where they'd be called by their names.
As Caddis emerging, they broke the surface tension
skimming wingless, in dancing shoes across the water
their mother-stitched dresses jingling.

Young prophets of the quality of rivers
reach down and help us up
we try to remember the last words you heard us say
before jumping into the Moon and flying away.

Or field and postal workers
who leave no leaf unturned
laboring in the treasure house
where neither moth nor rust destroys.

Amidst the crowd, a woman from Ball Club
found him and knew of his sorrow
She gathered him up, he hardly knew her,
she said, "This happens to us all the time."
I fear not
I fear not
I fear not the vigil
Inescapable, dust blowing away
The bough and the bush burn too bright
Thorn beat to fiber, growing back to rose
his grief gave way to white light.

THE WISDOM OF BEES
Lynda Ferguson

The wisdom of bees tells us to
enjoy the flowers while we work;
it makes the job easier
and the honey sweeter.

The tiniest of wings can lift up
the heaviest of things.

It's good to dance when we greet friends;
it improves our memories,
makes the stories of our travels more interesting,
and creates a lasting impression.

When in the presence of a bee, expect visitors;
sweetness attracts company.

LAMENT
Lynn Fena

> *summer grass aches and whispers*
> *with your presence — Carl Sandberg*

your absence cries between each blade
not silent now
thrusts up to my face

to face each summer day
grass must bear the weight of others
absorb the rain
must give out oxygen for those who walk upon it
must wake to its season without sleep

I lament the space between us
full of the sound that is not word, not music, not noise —
sound of light flickering between greens
sound of wind died down
sound above flat water
sound between the sound of things
your sound in my life now

still, the hum of your breathing within my chest

REDEFINING REVERENCE
Maggie Kazel

I choose to homechurch my kids
and make this morning hallowed
by abandoning the dishes,
letting clump, those papers and possessions
letting travel, in triumphant herds,
all dust bunnies and
all measures
of time and pace

It's a sleepy religion, that takes much practice
to redeem and to savor
So I am in my jammies, praying to this coffee cup,
telephoning putter litany
with another of our crew...
the children chorus in their sacred giggles
over some one thing, then everything —
it's these days, of all souls in sleep-gear,
all sainted and allayed
when there's no *Hallelujah!* for the glorious choices
we have and have not made,
no *Glory Be!* for minutes strung together,
the ordinary twinkling lights of an ordinary day,
we solitary parents
shepherd in these lowly places
these places where we really matter
where no one comes often,
by accident or design

I give my silent Praises
for the chores left unhurried and undone
Praises for the simplest breakfast
everyone found all on their own
Amen! for the slow and simple
Amen! for this soft, warm and delicious
Amen! for those pets who want me to stay put and petting
Amen! for these kids who go on endless make-believing

My redemption the kind most easy to be missed
with these faithful in their p.j.s, padding softly 'round in grace,
blessed to be together, in our small and sleepy haze
the fire and the brimstone, left so very long ago,
we quiet, close, and deep contented,
reverent of each other, and humble by default
in our soulful little chapel
we are the holiest of families,
we are a holy
holy *us*

UNTITLED
Maggie Kazel

Oh, and the prayer!
Gold wings fan
Me into deliverance...
My hands make ready
For flight / Say the word
And I shall be
Healed, healing and on my way...

FROM BIRDS
Marce Wood

I have found
so many
feathers
recently.
What could it mean
other than
it's time
to fly?

LUCAS
Margaret Veeder

You were born at the end of a nine-hour, grip-the-steering-wheel, light-a-candle-in-the-church drive. You were amazement handed over in a thin, blue blanket with a red stocking cap. Who knew what unawakened joy my heart could hold? Who knew that the shimmering golds and burnished oranges of that fall could be even more breathtaking because one tiny hand outstretched toward ours?

Now, I'm the grandma who sings French drinking songs and anthems as lullabies. I'm the grandma who sends sugar-flecked cookies. I'm the one who buys two sets of books — one for your end of the phone, one for mine. I'm the grandma at the other end of the spoon of heaping wild rice cereal. I'm the one who holds you and rocks you, who doesn't put you down and won't let you down. Not while there's life in me.

Your favorite word is "more." More milk, more songs, more blueberries, more sand beaches, more slides to climb. When I think about you, "more" is the word that most often comes to mind because I too want more. More stories to read, more baths to draw for you to splash in, more Minnesota border boat rides, more time with you, more years to watch you grow, more life.

In your blue eyes, I see the answers to all the questions I've ever asked. In your laugh, I know the best blessing of a lifetime of blessings. Taking care of myself becomes a priority because I want to see you become you. Being true to myself becomes urgent because I want you to know me. The grandma at the end of the world, and it's your world now.

On that sun-splayed September day, a new life was born. Mine.

BIOLUMINESCENT BAY
Marie Zhuikov

You ask me if I
can dance.
I lie
and say no.
I glide
bioluminescent
in the water, warm
among the starfire
that brings heaven
home.

The spirits of my friends
wink in and out
trail down my arms
as I lift them
from the water,
a belly dancer gesturing,
longing for the lost ones.

I float with them,
turn and spin
around and around
to the music
pounding from the boat
until I am dizzy
with memory.
Salt tears commingle
drip back
to the sea.

You are a bright star
overhead
alive and vital
full of possibilities
that are innocent enough
or not,
I do not know yet.

Star
streak down with me
into the night,
into the Caribbean Sea.
Churn the water
and watch the
sparks fly
with our dance
of life.

ALL DAY THE SKY ABOVE
Mark Maire

A blue and gold day, a spring Saturday,
and the poison of a week left behind
leaves the body, so slowly does it leave.

The road weaves between birch trunks, iced inlets,
freshets that gush across sheltered black slants.

Soon but not yet come the red-letter days:
long, stately windows approached like altars,
opened wide at long last for sun and warmth;
the mind and heart clear as big glass bells,
all day the sky above permanent blue.

ADOPTION HOMEWORK
Michelle Matthees

Her chair burns a hole through the floor.
She's picked it up and slammed it down
so many times she's scraped an exit.

Fuck the varnish, she says, fuck the sun.
I'm telling you the truth, she says,
and you can't make me believe that

two and two are four. "Five, five, five"
forces the chair. Equal sign equals
sucker, and I ponder cause and

effect and people without wounds.
The scab on the floor increases.
Each year the opened wood bleached as cream

darkens into a vast puddle. Imagine moving
on, I say, the next word problem,
figure your own house simple and quiet,

the white refrigerator with food.
You can choose about the fence.
Go ahead. Believe in things making sense.

Trust me, the teacher will accept your answer.

DIVORCE
Michelle Matthees

Canoeing through snow down the road.
This is a precursor for dreams of flood.

Why? The mind makes
its own season and accommodates.

The strangeness of this is beyond reproach,
restitution, government programs, balances.

Thirty-three, forty-four: the highways all have double names.
We will meet at the restaurant later.

The menu does not offer combination skillets with eggs.
I rise before the white film screen

where two women drive a small car underwater.
I lift my white placard half-way home.

I walk like a map unfolded in heavy wind,
flapping, flapping against

my face, my arms, my chest. I give myself over
to wind, tumble through washes, ditches, and gravel.

The mileage of the circulatory system is written in red.
When the melt comes, the returning blood of rivers

will still run blue and stain the plain
warring borders of our civil splitting flesh.

SUMMER AT THE 45TH PARALLEL WITHOUT YOU
Michelle Matthees

You are gone.
And it is only now that I look at you honestly,
through a new green leaf, say,
a translucent aspen spreading its thin palm.

It is summer,
not quite intense enough for me,
and night, like an upended kettle,
still swallows day at its close with a hollow hiss.

If the days could sear
particular brands upon my chest, if the raspberries
could stain my x-ray
I might forswear my loyalties toward your best season.

As it is
you are gone, and summer remains, neither youthful nor old, prime
time for action, not reflection
although the leaf lies on the surface of the water.

DIFFICULT TIMES
Michelle Matthees

The glob of ice cracked open
to reveal my grandfather's face.
Violently, it lay in the road,
tipped like the aftermath of a riot.

The day was gray, and people
were not looking very close into it.
Broken bits of carrot stained
the salted sewer drains.

Past his countenance, I tread,
past the smashed carrots.
My hand touched my own face
as I wept, walking on.

THE YEAR IN FLOWERS
Micky McGilligan

Tulips
Green, green, green spikes growing
then suddenly yellow, red, purple, pink
and gone too soon.
Green again to brown
melding back to soil
for another year.

Marigolds
Yellow, orange shining
small but powerful in scent
offending rabbits
pleasing the eye
all summer into fall.

Gladiolas
Green stalks for months it seems
then a show of shows begins
in late August
tall stems of multiple blooms
every color except blue
the flaming passion
culmination of summer.

Asters
Last to bloom
before the frost
a month maybe two
of sturdy purples and blues
whites and pinks
last chance to seize the season
til snow puts you all to sleep
until tulips force themselves up
everyone beginning again.

WEATHER AND MEMORY
Molly Tillotson

Sometimes as I exit the house and enter the world of a Minnesota winter, the north wind pulls the breath from my mouth like a soundless, inside-out gasp. When this happens and my lungs feel the sudden depletion, I remember every first morning in McMurdo. Antarctica is a place of cold winds and the buildings of McMurdo Station create windy tunnels that make buildings seem wrong and completely necessary. I remember pausing to find my breath; where did it go? There is so much space; I turn toward the wind to fill my lungs and turn back to literally save face as tears freeze and thaw on warm skin. Even among dull metal buildings, (we are like so much stored cargo here), I can feel the expanse that is Antarctica. It is like the way I feel the presence of Lake Superior eight miles from my home in the woods. But the lake offers orientation and Antarctica does not. This continent that is confused about where it stops and the ocean starts infuses me with the same: the wind blows past me, through me, becomes my posture. I turn to keep my breath from being sucked away; I am back.

I remember skiing along completely occupied with the soft puffs from Mount Erebus, the wind in my ears and my own thoughts when the volcano disappeared and I was transported unexpectedly to another world. I felt my home. I was sensually aware of a strong missing — what was it? Thick fog had rolled in like night falling. I was surrounded by something I had forgotten to miss and I missed it with all of my cells. I stopped and remembered darkness, closeness, the privacy of night. I wanted to stay right there in that dense freezing fog; it was time to go home.

Every year I considered staying in Antarctica longer. My job was to move fuel by pipeline, truck, plane, and ship as well as miles of temporary hose that stretched across a seasonal ice sheet; there was always more work. But it was time at home that was truly not long enough. The last weeks before leaving for Antarctica were predictably frenzied. I was acutely focused and scattered at the same time. It was unlike me. There was always too much to get done of course but it was more that there was too much to feel. One year I stopped on the way to the airport to see my goddaughter. She was little then, maybe four, and as I left and looked back through the cab window I saw her reaching for me then clutching her heart and my heart broke but I continued; I left. An ice friend, Judy, told me how she always cried for the first two weeks on the ice. I didn't. She had been going to Antarctica for a dozen years or more. I was fresh and new and full of denial.

I imagined working seasonally at the bottom of the world forever until one summer I knew I wouldn't. It could have been the transitions in McMurdo: my job was becoming more stressful and less fun; my social circle was changing. I was not excited to go back. Or it could have been the changes at home: I was in love, out of debt and many things seemed possible. But I think looking back that it was the maturing of a deeper realization in my psyche. I recognized the destruction to relationship (to people, to place, to my own identity) that was inherent in my constant state of arriving and leaving. Transition is a place all its own and it is possible to simply stay in it and never be fully in the place where you stand.

NURSING A NEWBORN WITH ONLY STREETLIGHTS ON
Moriah Erickson

I palm your head,
your gummy, velvet cranium
that is a perfect
puzzle piece, ball-in-socket
fit to my hand, pushing you toward
my naked skin. I feel

the tear of your talons
at me, the chaos of flailing limbs
as I aim the spraying arrow
of my nipple at the shadow-cavern,

your open, frantic mouth.
Through the window, I watch
customers come and go from the laundromat

up on Calvary Road while you suck.
Snow in wisping
whirls knocks the tops
off the stacks of perfectly
folded towels. I feel

my carpals click beneath your china-thin scalp, watch
your blue-black eyes flick from side to side, seeing
nothing, as you drift off
to silken, violet baby-dreams. You release

your powerful death-
suck, the one that makes me gasp.
I raise you to my shoulder, a sentinel, upright
and pound your fragile back.

The silver of the streetlight
turns your ancient bone face
even paler, the white-blue

trickle, the only thing
I have left to give you, leaks from the cornice

of your slack mouth.
You raise your frizzled brows

in an almost sleep-smile, remembering
what you were before
you were mine.

WHAT I WANT
Moriah Erickson

I want a red dress.
I want a small waist and big
exotic eyes, the kind that get noticed.
I want men to swoon
when I speak because of *what* I say.
I want you
to stop and wait for me
when I fall behind, distracted
by the scent of lilacs or the pile of dogshit
that resembles someone
we both know.

I want to wear flannel shirts. I want
to shed this skin
and wade into the water. I want
to sit around the campfire.
I want to laugh and be certain
it isn't too loud, it doesn't make me ugly.

I want to touch all your right places,
my hands made of peacock feathers, lithe
and vibrant. I want
to flood you with the red
of my dress, comfort you with the plaid
of my flannel shirt. I want
to erode away all the girls
you loved before me, the pretty ones
you can't forget.

I want lakes of fire
in my thighs, so I can sear my name on you,
make you wear
my name
the same way I wear yours.

WANDERER
Moriah Erickson

Clarence goes looking
for his bride
along the riverbank where she liked
to collect pocketfuls
of clamshells with their oil-slick rainbow insides
gleaming empty in the sun.
He has forgotten
to tell the door-warden
at his assisted living home, forgotten
his wife is dead six years now, forgotten
the river sludge has dimmed her
radiant mollusks to brown. He picks
his way home late, past
dark, past the last bus.
His trousers are slashed
with mud, snagged by brambles. His hair
is matted with worry
beneath his tweed fedora.

Clarence cannot respond
where he has been when the desk-lady
asks, her face a map
of concern. He is consumed
with the idea of his wife,
his Claudine,
out wandering alone
along the riverbank
so late at night.

FISHING ON LAKE SUPERIOR
Moriah Erickson

Huddled in the bow
of the little flat-bottom jon
boat, I pull my rain gear
around my bones tight
to keep the spray out.
I watch my uncle
hunched in the back
steer with the tiller, his brown hand
ashen in the flat light of morning.
The little boat splits the water
leaves a white fading
trail in the steely grey
chopped weeds churn up in the wake.
A loon surfaces, following, hopeful.
The growl of the motor
bites my ear.
The sun has not broken
from beneath the edge
of the lake, a pink cast colors
the undersides of the clouds.
"Red sun in morning" my old
aunt warned as we shuffled out
after bowls of steaming oatmeal,
and digging worms with aching fingers.
Lures rattle against the side
of the boat, our poles tight with line,
the loon circling, its red eyes
hungry, searches the water
for discarded fish.

YOU CAN HAVE THE CROCUSES
Nance O'Brien

You can have the crocuses,
Croaking and coughing up Spring,
Brash violet lah-dee-dahs
Of the first wiley sunwarm days.

You can have the dapper dafs,
Satchels of sunshine,
Jumped-up jazz band of snazzmeisters
Standing in their self-made spotlight.

You can have the tulips too,
Tongue-flapping gossipers agape,
Their indecisive palette
Of swaying promises.

Give me the forget-me-nots,
Green, deep green for days, and slow to other color,
As shy in their lazy shade they slip
Into the blue of the sky they look up to.

ONE ORANGE, MARCH SNOW
Pamela Mittlefehldt

bowl of orange slices
scarred wooden table
March snow
beyond winter weary windows

another latitude
in the light
tropical sun
glows
in each sweet segment
prism
refracting the pewter day
citric mist
twists with woodsmoke and snowdrift

each bite
thaw and flow
rivulets of snowmelt
spring rain

monsoons sweep
through the
glazed spruce
daffodils tremble
in the sultry heat

enough for now
brisk zest
of hope

FOOD
Pamela Mittlefehldt

Taste a tomato,
relish the flesh, the juice, the red —
let summer slide down your throat.
Name it
and speak in tongues:
Nahuatl: *tomatl*

Savor a potato,
grainy cream, earthy grit of skin —
fill your mouth with memory, migration.
Name it
and claim new worlds:
Taino: *batata*

Lily, nightshade, fungus, gourd —
we risk them all:
tug roots from common ground,
harvest the polyglot garden,
fill baskets with leaf and seed,
bulb and stalk —
the lexicon of hunger and desire —
an edible alphabet:
> beet, kale
> okra, pea —
the heat of jalapeño,
the grammar of greens.

Sample a yam,
mine the golden motherlode —
it isn't ore that feeds desire
but bread, fruit, food.
Name it
and bestow a bounteous benediction:
Fulani: *nyami*.

Eat.

FIVE-HAIRED BEARD OF WISDOM
Pamela Mittlefehldt

She would not pluck them,
those yellowed hairs crimped on her chin —
a terrible beauty
no one would call venerable.
Homely, ancient,
she gazed at the face
hooked in the tarnished mirror,
a wavering prism —
the scratched surface
refracting her life:
brown irises,
eyebrows like torn rags,
wrinkles rising —
feathers
tipping her face toward the light.
She nodded,
neither pleasure nor disgust,
studied the arc
of rainbow and rust.

ANOTHER IRIS
Pamela Mittlefehldt

> *It doesn't have to be the blue iris...*
> *— Mary Oliver, "Praying"*

It doesn't have to be the blue iris —
take a dandelion,
sunsplat serendipity of spring,
or the tight-fisted lilac nubs,
releasing a universe of green
when rolled between winter-weary fingers.

The promise isn't glory,
but the simple relief
of
agreement:

after ice, ecstasy.

It doesn't have to be the ocean —
take the windruffed puddle
at the foot of the drive,
stand on its shore,
seek the far horizon.

GENERATIONS
Peggy Trojan

My youngest holds
her daughter
with strong, certain hands,
talking slowly,
making bonds.

When I was young,
and she was new,
did I hold her so?
Did I whisper
near her tiny ear,
"Welcome. Welcome."?

IN THE SAME BOAT
Penny Perry

his hands wrap the oars like thumbless paws
he spots on the treeline behind me
perfectly able to look through my being
bringing the handles to his chest
he rows
smoothing a delay in each draw

I only breath as the oars come up
keeping still as they fold underwater
slicing into the dark airless deep
with just the memory of light in the sky
we are ghosts of a kind
each transparent to a horizon
in a seamless glide away from shore

GOODBYES
Penny Perry

it helps to be familiar with the dirt
that fills a loved one's grave
the slice and thrump of each shovel turn
a rhythm that matches fresh grief
with this last tending
I give them back to the ground
back to themselves without me

HEALING
Penny Perry

my dear friend is transforming an old hurt
an old hurt to a young self
just now seen with fearless eyes

during the night
swallows fly to her
busy to pull golden threads
from a vestment she unknowingly still wears
each thread
unraveled and carried into the sky
is a too held breath

soon she breathes outside memory
the future drawn through her
like each precious filament

NORTH SHORE
Rocky Kiukanpi

there's a place where red willow grows
with orange sunrises and swallow songs
where the center of the world is everywhere
where fiction is real
alive in the waters
alive in the air
alive
that place where red willow glows
thru pipestone bowl
I let my spirit fly on trails of smoke cedar
whispering secrets of mother nature
she calls me her child
along the north shore
there's a place where red willow glows
where the center of the world is everywhere

WHAT WARD PREFERS
Ryan Vine

> *Some (the delicate ones) judging the spectacle cruel*
> *will prefer to die.* — Carlos Drummond de Andrade

So, Ward is a delicate one, hardened
and softened by what life is not.
And where are you, Carlos, rough, old poet?
Ward knows he prefers something, but death
seems too harsh, too final, too finito, and who is anyone
to say no more Ward. Besides, he has his fear
of commitment keeping him from suicide.
And he has his ego, whose wheels are still
sometimes so big that whole weeks
may be traversed in days. He has — what?
His time? His health? He has many years
lived a young man with an old and wounded heart,
the memories of his women wandering its empty hallways,
clapping their sandaled heels along its floors.
Yes, days now to Ward are like doors to walk through,
and yes he knows tragedy is god — how many people
had he met who were made by it? But prefer to die?
Prefer the dirt beneath? What do you know, Carlos —
what can you know — of any suffering but your own?

SNOWBANK SHERPA
Ryan Vine

The mountain doesn't know
when you're trying to climb it,

and the world around it
doesn't wait for you to finish.

Ward the Snowbank Sherpa
says this is his first edict.

The second: watch your step.
Because if you fall from here

you'll fall forever.
See, at this altitude darknesses

are easily mistaken
for substance, and any pains

you may have will appear
as people, dark silhouettes

always approaching, always
climbing up behind you.

At summit, we'll be six feet higher
than the streets of Duluth,

and when cars pass, notice
their headlights roll below us

before their sound. Notice
the streetlight's hum.

People will accuse you
of being high, and you may feel

lightheaded. Listen: I want you
to know, if something should happen,

no one can save us up here.

127

WARD'S RULE 5
Ryan Vine

if at a Christmas party
you should walk into a room

and see the woman you love
sharing a bench with another man

leaning over her crossed legs
and into her laugh

to avoid detection
for god's sake don't shuffle

just crawl into your pants
hands first through your pockets

WITHOUT NEED
Ryan W. Keller

My daughter asked a question
at her grandmother's funeral.
She said the man spoke of heaven,
a place without need.
Being only four,
she looked happy
when she asked if we could visit.
I told her yes, but after many years,
because that's what Grandma wanted.
Saddened, she asked if she could look
through the glass and wave,
so Grandma would know she was okay.
I told her the sky was not glass but air.
She told me Grandma is not in the sky.
So I asked where?
Grandma is in a place without need.
Grandma went to the grocery store.

GRANARIES OVERFLOW
Ryan W. Keller

If love could be thrashed or milled,
picked or baled, combined or stored,
we'd always be hectic with harvest
on a farm not loaned and leveraged
for tractors with peeling paint,
and trucks crumbling with rust.

On our horizon the cloud bank always looms.
Lightning storms keeping phones off hook
and threatening to close our shutters.

If love was measured by stock or yield,
book reports wouldn't be written with red pens
stolen from our bank's loyalty and reward table.
If love could be brought from field to market,
we would buy our children the choice
of doing homework in black ink.

ELEMENTS
Sheila Packa

All winter, as I kindled the fire
my body burned
days on end, not sexual but acrid
at the stake
the little girl kept by her father at the table
to finish her dinner
adolescent selves
the wives I was, a conflagration
smoke
my own immolation
of the past.
At the end, a bear, turned to charcoal
and ash
carried to the icy road
all winter
back and forth
I spoke with the tongues of flames.

At night I tied myself to the sound
of your breathing
the waves of in- and exhalation
on dream's shore
pulled up my boat and walked
on the moonlit strand
away
from the flames of cold and heat
mornings when the world came back, floated
upon the surface
of the light, next to your face, resurrected
and lost my self
tossed my ash into the waters
in vapor and ice and free.

Trees felled
tunnels bored through the mountain
my body, bull-dozed, all the earth
another word for gravity, stone
crags, granite faces, ledges lifted by glacier

and left, carried by trains
iron strip-mined
weathered
worn by the rivers that spring
from underground
with eruptions and slides, floods, quakes
lightning strikes

made into shadow
eclipsed.
I have been traveling in all directions
with wind
battered by relentless force
worn by irreconcilable differences
borne out

into the space of our hands
that take from this life
and give to the wind our breath
with the strings of an instrument
give to the flames
give to the water, give to the earth.

ENOUGH DESTINATION
Sheila Packa

Gray pigeons of the hospital parking ramp
flap wings on the i-beams
over the thunk thunk of car doors
nest in shadows above retreating footsteps
never crossing
the threshold of double doors to find out
how five empty wheelchairs
wait in a vacant pink corridor

count neither loss nor gain
or wonder who or what Staff Only admits
laundry or morgue or emergency generators
scale the faces of concrete
never to need more light than this
nor pause before elevator doors
reminded of a mother who foundered on 3 or 5

stroll over painted yellow lines
live whole lives ignoring ambulance drivers
call to patients or visitors
distracted by other news
brood on eggs that hatch
and fledge undetected
on banks of video monitors.

MEMORY / THE MINE
Sheila Packa

I return but it's all excavation — me
an employee of the organization.
I remember a long road past a gate,
a dead landscape.
Dust. Noise. First the crusher and then
where I worked, the agglomerator
with its conveyors to the trains.
First stop, the dry.
A sink like a Roman fountain.
Clothes blackened by taconite, yellow and white
hard hats, coveralls, steel toed boots,
safety glasses, the whistle
starting and stopping each shift.
For this, I'd propped myself on a ledge
for the paycheck.
Steel beams, high voltage. Dripping grease.
One of the crew leaning on high pressure
water hoses, blowing dust out of the nose
into a handkerchief, pushing spillage
down the sloping concrete floors
below rolling furnaces,
swallowing free salt tablets from dispensers.
On a swing shift, counting
days till the long weekend
taking smoke breaks, and calculating
what falling asleep on graveyards might cost.
All night and day the trains came to load
and carry to the ore docks.
In the lunch room took from my lunch pail
a paperback. Kept myself awake
with coffee from my thermos.
Avoided the pellets and their third degree burns.
stared into the middle distance
not the ends but the means —
the first place I'd worked below the surface.

134

MAKING A LIVING IN SOCIAL WORK
Sheila Packa

So much suffering in the world is unearned
wrongfully assigned, accidental —
I walk up the stairs and in a dark hallway knock.
The leather of my boots mean to break
from the soles. Salt and grit on the floor.
Sometimes it doesn't answer — sometimes
        a band of sun under the door
lights faraway music. So much is exacted,
re-enacted, swift and shrewd. I know its name
the sound of faucets and drains.
In the book of disappointments nowhere fresh paper.
But even here doors open in greeting
lead and follow to an ash covered table
amid smoke, hinge beginning on ending.

EMERGENCE
Shelley Getten

For a long time
you hang
in a back bend,
half in, half out
of a papery shell —
brown skin of
the underground
creature you were.

Slowly, new legs
reach for bark,
you climb
out of the lifeless crust,
of your old body,
and a new tail pulls free.

You are not
in a hurry,
but in less than an hour
become a new thing —
Cicada —
with large inquisitive eyes
and delicate, fairy wings —
wet pieces of crumpled plastic wrap
that unfold into iridescent beauties.

At this moment of change,
more elegant
than ever —

you glisten —
gold,
yellow,
green.

THREADS
Sherry Rovig

First you wore it
then you passed it on
mended
or stored in the cold room
until the style came back
(She said it always did)
We gathered
on the day appointed
went through the boxes
again
either grew to the next wardrobe,
repacked or consigned to the rag box
Saying farewell to worn-out favorites

We cleaned out their house first
saving the things Mom would need in her apartment
Years later, we cleaned out her apartment
and found homes for most of it
I took a bag of rags to use in my shop
and it was my undoing
No way could I use her old nightgown
For the life of me,
I can't even use Dad's old T shirts
for anything but tears

I handed out Mom's embroidered hankies
at the memorial service
Thankfully, there were many to share
She always had one tucked in a sweater pocket
Now, I always have one with me

It's the sewn-on name labels that made it harder
Dungarees and suspenders giving way
to the sweat pants and shoes with Velcro fasteners
we bought him after the stroke
I can wear the paint-spattered jean jacket with the corduroy collar,
too shabby to take to the care center
So much easier without that name tag

to carry his strength with me

A package arrives
with Dad's old blue flannel robe
We pass it to the one who needs it next
Now, ready to wrap me
in the memory of his arms

LIGHTNING
Stephanie Kessler

Sitting on the floor:
Our backs pushed to the bunk beds.
Our knees pulled to our chests.

She read.
I imagined.

A horse named Lightning.
A safe time with Mom.

The pages turned too fast for me.
The end came much too soon.

I wanted more of Lightning.
I wanted more of Mom.

The words I barely remember.
The story I hardly know.

There were no other horses.
There was no time for stories.

Lightning was a special horse.
The first horse with my Mom.

WITHOUT WORDS
Susan Hawkinson

The tall trees shrunk to stalks of broccoli
as we lifted off the runway,
my father reclining behind the controls.
He set the dials and turned down the radio.
No place in mind, nowhere we had to go, so —
he pointed to a lake. I mouthed the name.
He raised his eyebrows twice. I did the same.

We followed each other's fingers
across the windows of the Cessna
to the world's largest open-pit mine
and beyond to forests cradling unnamed ponds
where loons nested and fought with eagles
for the lives of their young.
He pointed to a lake. I mouthed the name.
He raised his eyebrows twice. I did the same.

All afternoon we glided along
happily too warm in the cockpit calm,
wings parallel with the terrain —
Lake Winnibigoshish, Cutfoot Sioux,
Mississippi River, Waboose Bay.
I pointed to a lake and mouthed its name.
He raised his eyebrows twice. I did the same.

Cessna 2132 Romeo — my father's 182 —
flew us like lost children over Bitterwater Slough,
Pokegama, Hale, the Kawishiwi River,
waters we loved as we loved each other
without words, which were dicier
than the oncoming weather.
I pointed to the lightning and mouthed its name.
We raised our eyebrows twice and ended the game.

"2132 Romeo to tower. Over."
"Tower to Romeo. Over."
"We're coming in. Over."
"All clear, Romeo. Over and out."
"Over and out." I mouthed the refrain.
He circled the airport and landed the plane.

MIGRATION
A poem in two voices
Susan Hawkinson &
Loree Miltich

Embarking

Some of us are always seeking water
            Some of us stay home
Boiling Lake
180 to 197°
            our journeys internal, domestic
195 feet but not the bottom
            Forced by experience
wherever we go
Dominica, Lesser Antilles,
            to grapple with what's foreign,
grayish-blue water bubbling up
            a feeling that challenges
in a cloud of vapor
            all we thought we knew,
this boiling cauldron
            assaults our senses
            and we've embarked, spun off

A trek to get there
13 K. from the nearest road
            unbound from familiar
past sulfur springs, over mountains
through gorges
            and fear
across the Valley of Desolation
            to transformation

Across the backyard
                    "I didn't know it was dangerous"
early morning off the dock
steam rises from the lake, July air
                    Family become strangers
46° calls my father
                    separate souls we see for the first time

Snorkeling
through lily pads and reeds
                    Chance encounters
Largemouth Bass and their shadows
                    that trigger pictures from the past
deadheads
                    stacked in layers of meanings,
touching down in
                    messages from those nearly forgotten
foot sucking muck
                    shape-shift sense we thought we'd made
                    habits of seeing no longer work
kicking ocean waves with fins
suddenly swimming
                    "You've felt this, I'm certain"
across flat water
over the ocean wall, 1000 foot freefall,
                    untethered
whirlybirding
                    in desperate hope
                    of new understanding
it's still water

The Long Flight

Hummingbirds balance on the line
                Evolutionary biologists explain,
between clothes pins and feeder
                it's preparation, persistence
poised to fly south for winter
                fervent attention
fueled with insects and nectar
                to greater purpose

In trees along the way
                The phone rings, bad news
they slip into a state of torpor
                voices come unbidden
when they sleep, some awaken
                mystery turns the heart
upside down
                and the journey begins

Revving up their wings
                Sky-clogging flocks
from 50 to 500 in the morning
                of last words, lost dreams,
off they go again
                pulsing ruby-throated beauty
for five to ten days until
                memories stored in muscle
                wait like little birds for release
they reach the Gulf
navigating their night flight by stars
Each bird must take this trip alone
                "I miss you already"

Flying in the company of others offers no protection
    New landscapes and language come
Predators don't bother
    as comfort fades off in the distance
with so small a prey
    Not as instinctual as birds,
Only one at a time
    What is the *must* of our migration?
can sip from the flower's lip
    the reason we make this trip?

Flying alone presents adventure
    It will lure you out, or simply come
one misses in a flock
    and take you
when conversations from home
    amaze you, even with time, repel
travel abroad, undisturbed
    Staying unchanged, impossible
by foreign words
    though journey's end still uncertain

Hummingbirds make this pilgrimage
    taking such risk for unknown reward
twice a year, testament to life force
    Trust. Telluric currents will guide you
No hesitation
    "Just gonna get there"
Each must go back to the source

Return

Edward Abbey wrote:
This is the most beautiful place on earth.
There are many such places.
Every man, every woman carries in heart
and mind the image of the ideal place
known or unknown, actual or visionary.
For me, I'll take...

the fringe of steam still on the far shore
                    Big Water, Dakota prairie,
Sun has not yet burned the stand
                    New York City's glint,
of paper birch, bright white
                    wherever *you* are...

Overhead
                    Each are called
a pair of crows caw
                    and must respond
as they jet
                    fearfilled, into foreign country
through jackpine
                    toward strength, untested
                    learning what we lack
Leaves in the front yard
                    Tempered by a thousand trials
lie face down
                    Some paint and pray
in the frost
                    Some don't come back

Here
                    Somewhere
the heart is
yet
                    wandering,
                    you may find your way home,
somewhere
                    set down your sack and cross
another hemisphere
                    the threshold
                    If you return,
Blue footed booby birds parade
                    bring a boon back for us
in their desert island dance
                    bells and scarves, stories
Penguins,
                    so rare they have no names
stuntmen of the Galapagos,
torpedo beneath the waves
                    World remade
of their Pacific
home
                    renewed
is where they plant their blue feet
                    See how lightly you can live
black fur shimmering with water

BLESSINGS
Susan Niemela Vollmer

Today I count the winter sun
Peeking between bare birch trees
and through the kitchen curtains

Today I count the cardinal
raising its liquid notes
over the rumble of trucks on the street

Today I count the yeasty scent
of bread rising on the counter
gently pushing its cloth cover higher

Today I count your steps
across the wooden deck
striding over the threshold

CHANGES
Susan Niemela Vollmer

When we were children
the mine pit was huge, open, and off limits
We accepted without thinking
words like dry house and B shaft

With our classmates and cousins
we had dads who worked in the mines
graveyard shift, afternoon, or days
and always had ore-red hands

Now the mine pits
have turned into lakes
the underground mine into a science lab
the dry house into a museum

And we have turned
into generations with futures
in distant places and different lives
with roots still firm in the rusty soil

MARIA NEEDS A MOTHER IN THE SPRINGTIME
Tera Freese

To ring the morning bells of myth and miracle,
to sing to her of lake and sun, of ice
retreating, first ship in the harbor,
shake out the quilts, oh cedar of praise.

Maria needs a mother in the springtime
to carry her to fast speaking rivers,
to encourage her bare feet to feel
cool grasses, hot stones, streams of snow melt.

To point out the two hawks
dancing circles in the day sky, to tell her
it is significant, these birds returning to us.

Maria needs a mother in the springtime
to search foggy trails for first pussy willows,
the rise of their soft growth touched
to her lips, the lids of her eyes.

To celebrate with jade her first blood
to tie bright ribbons from her wrists
teach her the buried chants of goddess
spin her in all of the secret pockets of warmth.

THE MASTER OF A FLUTE
Tera Freese

The heart of a warrior is no longer a work of
art, all of its stars have fallen asleep,
we all were in love with god at the birthing hour.

This is what I press into the lap of the planet,
the eyes of youth turn from a bright interior,
here is a nudge from your mother, move on.

Who is the master of a flute, the breath or the fingers,
our question points to bombs and mirrors, what shattered
this is busy stringing beads on a medicine pouch.

Mother, I have forgotten which of the saints to pray to
when something is lost, if only we had not tossed
the ashes of your knowledge to the salty ocean.

Instead of returning to the inn, remove your
shoes and the dirty rope from around the mare's neck,
so many have already kissed the forest goodbye.

THE RAFT
Tera Freese

It would be easier
if there were someone to blame,
this leader or that group of officials,
the green branch torn from its tree,
that final blue weave of sky.

We all know the difficulties of being human,
some storm always leaving or arriving.
Fear claps its bright red palms over
the hundredth psalm, while children
continue to plough bravely from the womb.

How did we arrive here?
Who beaded this pattern on a slow winter's loom,
dreamed up the cosmos, that dark patch
of pigment on my newborn's thigh.

What is needed — an ocean of sacrifice —
to return this constellation
to the night, to reverse a fossil,
from that thimble of ashes,
to resurrect a single song.

Can you really say that you have not found
a single teaching
to grow your compassion?
Then — take the raft —
It is waiting in all of the wild dogwood
by Ophelia's river.

THIS RECURRING KINDNESS
Tera Freese

Every August it happens
white blaze of afternoon
ripens the fruit
makes even the birds
fat as queens.

Here they are now
twittering and thrashing in the high
sweet grasses, dark wings dusted
with deep gold pollens
throwing confetti of fireweed
days of merriment and feasting.

Even in their tiny eyes —
a bright exuberant health
as in something that has come 'round again
to meet its full potential.

These are the same mourning doves
that eat dark oily seed
from my pale palm after the curtain
of Autumn has dropped.

Yes, even when there is not this bounty,
there is still enough.
For that which dwells in the first hung star
is there, too, in the last to fade
to morning's tide.

MOTHER'S DAY SONNET
Teresa Alto

Thursdays were Bookmobile nights in those days.
Grabbing our piles of books from the shelf, Mom
and I strolled in the afternoon rays
in the quiet town far from Vietnam.
I knew nothing of that war, but I shared
a goal Mom had as a girl: to read all
the books on this library's shelves; we cared
about all there was to know, heard the call
of every title embossed on a spine,
thought that the next one might tell us the tale
we most needed to hear then, I in my
child's naivety that I could inhale
it like popcorn, and she knowing our aim
a futile one, but noble, worth the game.

TRAINING WHEELS
Teresa Alto

Dad wasn't too steady on a bike himself,
     yawping in a sympathetic cadence to my wobble.

Tongue out, I swung the red frame side to side

        reaching now the angle of repose
           now the point of no return.
Until, undulations decreasing,
    momentum all with me now,
        I rushed toward the breathy world.

     Each square of concrete a bumpy step leading
     wherever I was going to go.
Fast.

INDOOR MIGRANTS
Teresa Boyle Falsani

I'm like a cat,
my friend says, telling me
how she follows the December sun
chair to chair,
room to room,
uprooting herself
as warm spots of light
drift backwards — west to east
across the carpet.
She carries books and newspapers,
a bag of knitting, a notebook
to write lists, and now,
the telephone.

The sun blinks through tangled
barbed wire trees around my house,
its arc too low to scale the tops
or heat anything
but captive inside air.
Well, I feel trapped, I answer,
pacing window to window,
searching the north sky
for one bright star
to lock down the bitter day.

Even a sliver of light
they say
can give a prisoner hope,
necessity of purpose
found in marking days.
I picture my friend at home
chasing her meager slice of sun
and wonder.
Compelled by unplowed roads
imperative as instinct,
we migrate inward,
sustained by simple miracles —
a telephone and glass.

156

FAITH

Terry Dunham

Walking away from the locked church in the wind, frustrated once again that the bulletin has no correlation with upcoming masses and that the outgoing phone message does not list the week's services, Jon catches motion in his peripheral vision and turns. A man across the usually busy 3rd Street shifts his weight back and forth, fussing with his suit while looking in the side mirror of a parked car.

He appears to be trying to attract Jon's attention, talking rather loudly to himself, tugging at his tie and glancing up, nearly catching Jon's eye. The flash of his glance averts slightly each time Jon looks his way, like a shy dog drawing someone near. His suit is a dated navy gabardine, shiny from wear, that bags a bit in the knees and puddles over the front of his shoes. He slips his necktie off over his head as Jon crosses the street in his direction.

"Can't seem to tie this thing right," the man says, as Jon approaches. "I'm heading to the DECC and I can't get it."

"Let me see, I'm pretty good with these."

"I think it matches," the man says.

"It does. Looks nice with the overcoat, too."

"Well, thank you."

"There. That looks sharp," Jon says as he ties the man's necktie properly and tightens it against the collar of his shirt, while a truck rumbles by and kicks up salt and gravel. "Happy Thanksgiving to you."

"To you, too. Thank you for your help!"

The man walks toward the corner, smiling. He waves and turns down the hill toward the city's soup-kitchen style Thanksgiving dinner. Jon stands for a while in the wind, watching the man's light step until his shape and movement become part of the backdrop of the city, and he is thankful he went to church this morning.

DREAM DRAWER
Theresa O'Halloran-Johnson

I

The desk is gone now, so is the mother who purchased it at a garage sale. Used, hardly at all though, for its sturdiness — it's heavy and functional — the drawers slide so smoothly and the small but capable fold-out table, and a 'secret drawer' that should have locked but didn't.

> *The desk will be taken to New York, Greenwich Village to be exact to host a typewriter and provide companionship to a St. Bernard while the girl plays out a reverse Mary Tyler Moore of sorts the girl huffed as she shouldered her side of the desk up the stairs.*

The desk is gone now, so is the mother, but the girl remains a secret un-lockable drawer inside the woman.

The desk never went east. It did go west thrice. To each edge of the prairie eastern and western, eastern edge twice.

It was cleaned out once by the man the girl calls husband. A violation of the desk, its contents, even the secret drawer is relegated to a cardboard box...

The desk is gone now, so is the mother, but the girl remains a secret un-lockable drawer inside the woman.

> *Distracted from their task of lifting and shifting the mother stopped and remarked upon the girl's pronouncement, "New York would be an awful big city for such a big dog to live."*

II

The desk is gone now, the girl remains though in a 'secret drawer' that should lock but can't.

The secret drawer holds found objects that will yield an important invention, plastic ink capsules, sharp pen nibs, calligraphy guides, matches, rolling papers.

The desk is gone now, so is the mother, but the girl remains a secret un-lockable drawer inside the woman.

Incredulous she is when the woman wakes at 2, 2:30 and 3 am to feed the voracious, restless, unappeasable 6 pounds 2 ounces of human.

Incredulous she is at the woman having another and another infant.

The ink cartridges replaced by pressed flowers, immunization records and secret paltry savings for something...

The desk is gone now, so is the mother, but the girl remains a secret un-lockable drawer inside the woman.

Incredulous she is as the woman sweeps the floor, hangs out diapers, makes love to her husband, and authorizes the sale of the desk from the garage, to move east,

not to New York.

The desk is gone now, so is the mother, but the girl remains a secret un-lockable drawer inside the woman.

CONCERNED
Tina Higgins

the finch
trapped in your garage   lives

lives so deeply
that she is compelled
to throw herself against the
bright light window panes
for one more chance

even she, so small   bird brained
recognizes entrapment, knows what
she is
missing
and will stop only when her small
so fragile, we think of them as soft,
bones   are broken
one by one
two by two
until she cannot go on

but even at this end
her spirit will still rally

dream of blooming sunflowers
safe, succulent boughs of pine needles
of song
to listen   and respond
call out with the thrill of knowing
she is never alone

she lives in the hum and drone of weeds
as they rub against each other
but the sound to her
does not grow old
it is another day
another day is all the reason she needs
to live again

when the wind is too strong
she seeks out her nest
a place she has struggled to build

inside, she huddles, lifts her feathers
like a shell and sleeps
cocooned among the night sounds

unattached
she will build another home
if wind, bullies, or fire
take this one   away

for the finch
I open the door, to be sure
I prop a heavy metal folding chair
against it
so the wind will not
suck another door closed

and I wait, like any other day,
for a flash of wing
for a glimpse of bright white
feather
to set me at ease

for the finch
I prepare an exit
watch her fly

for myself
I am not so concerned

WHEN THE FRUIT'S IN SEASON
Yvonne Rutford

The raspberries came in thick and heavy this year, bushes arching to the ground, and I go out to my field every day to pick them, and Sierra comes with me and she picks them too right off the bush, sometimes, or she waits for me to pick them for her and feed them to her, but if I get too absorbed in my own berrying she will wrestle her own off the stem with her teeth, and many of them fall to the ground, they are wedged and tangled in the grass beneath my feet, and her paws, and our soles may be berry-stained, stained red and sweet, there are so many this year, and now and then I think to myself I should collect them in a bucket, surely I could make something, a pie or jam or at least bring enough home to sprinkle on cereal or ice cream, but I don't, I eat them all right on the spot, as soon as they're in my hand they're in my mouth red and rain-washed and wild, and I realize there are people who would plan ahead and stash away, preserve the fruit for a future day, and these are the same people I am sure who have a savings account and a 401K, yes, I'm sure if they were here in this field they would have a bucket and they would be very careful about filling it before indulging in a taste or two, and me, I have no such preserves, I can't help but put the fruit in my mouth one by one or three by three as soon as it's ready, I just can't foresee the experience being as sweet when the sunshine and hot summer and thorn scrapes and berry stains and Sierra and I in this field are a distant memory.

BEDTIME PRAYER
Yvonne Rutford

The new moon, a fingernail clipping,
has set in the west, and earlier outside
in the cold dark glow of snow and stars
a Geminid meteor flashed its last radiance,
my breath made steam in the air, and all

was silent, and the dogs were dark shapes
I had to look away to see, since it is in peripheral
vision that light gathers and seeing in the dark
is possible. But now the lights are out and I
am tucked into flannel and goose down

and Sierra's soft solid back is pressed
against my shoulder, and I could lie awake
all night listening to her soft snore, imagining
where her wild dreams have taken her.
And two cats are curled on a red blanket

between my feet, another draped over my thighs,
and I feel the warmth and weight of all this,
I want to impress this moment into my being,
indelibly, into blood and flesh and bones
to make it permanent, retrievable. — I'm afraid

I don't live in the moment, but try to gather them
close, collect and hoard them, layer these moments
one upon another, a shield against dark days ahead,
that in the dark I may trace my fingers over my life
and know every crease, every curve.

NOTES ON CONTRIBUTORS
Alphabetized by First Name

Alissa Tran lives in northern Minnesota. She loves to read and write poetry that bends the rules. She is influenced by her studies in English and psychology. Additional influences include interests in culture, grief, travel, war, healing, dreams, language and reality. Occasionally she has the experience of percolating with a poem long enough to pour a cup of coffee without the editor getting in the way. Recent works have been influenced by transitions made within and through the body and an exploration of that inner space. Believing in the wisdom of the body, these poems voyage through — residing in the bones.

Amy Jo Swing knows about migration. She has lived in Alaska, Indiana, and Texas, but chose Minnesota as her home in 1996. She lives in Duluth with her partner and two daughters, not far from Lake Superior, which is a major source of inspiration as are the trees, rocks, animals, insects, and people. Amy Jo has an M.F.A. in poetry from Texas State University, San Marcos and currently teaches creative writing and composition at Lake Superior College.

Audrey L'Amie teaches writing to community college students in northern Minnesota during autumn, winter, and spring. Summers are saved for her own creative writing, which includes creative non-fiction, fiction, and poetry. When not teaching or writing, she enjoys reading, researching modern homesteading, and listening to audiobooks.

Bernadette Savage is a native of Cornucopia, Wisconsin and currently lives in Duluth, Minnesota. She is a retired teacher and counselor. Her poems have been published in *Dust and Fire, Loonfeather, Sistersong, The Wolf Head Quarterly,* and *North Coast Review*. She has studied poetry at the Prague Summer Residency Program in the Czech Republic and at the Madrid Summer Residency Program in Spain.

Bev Berntson was born in 1943 in St. Paul, MN. As a young adult she lived for short times in Crookston and Detroit Lakes, MN. She moved to Duluth, MN in 1968 and has called that home since then. She has four married children, five grandchildren, and lives with her husband, Jerry Challman. After leading the life of Mother, Nurse, and Elementary Educator, she has been born again as a Poet, Singer, and sometime Comedienne. "It's time to follow-up those 'first lines' that have been popping into my head since childhood," she says. She claims to have been strongly influenced by the Civil Rights movement, living in Hippie Communes, her Nighttime Dreamlife, Music, Reading, Family, Friends, and the study of Buddhist philosophy. She celebrates this as her first publication.

Beverly Hanks was born and raised in northern Minnesota. Her childhood was spent in Proctor, Minnesota with frequent visits to her grandmother's farm nearby.

Those experiences have been the inspiration of many of her stories. She now lives in Duluth and enjoys family, Nature, and the Lakewalk. Her stories have appeared in the *Greysolon Plaza Newsletter*. She also enjoys oil painting and her work has been displayed at the Proctor Federal Credit Union and the Lakeview Building in Duluth.

Bonita Sutliff was born and raised in Wisconsin. However, most of her adult years were spent in Minnesota. Since extended family members still live in the Menomonie area and she taught writing at UWS for the last 10 years, she considers herself a loyal Cheesehead! In her spare time she often strips and refinishes old furniture, for she enjoys freeing the wood of old paint or varnish and applying stain and new sealing agents to enhance the wood's natural beauty. When Bonita writes poetry, it is spontaneous and marks changes in her life.

Brooke Taylor Ballavance was born in August of 1995. She lives with her parents Brett and Adair and her sisters Tyler and Keara. Brooke is very involved in music playing both the alto saxophone and the guitar. She is also a writer. She started writing in 4th grade and continues to write both poetry and short stories. Brooke enjoys taking walks and hunting in the outdoors. She is a sophomore at Denfeld High School where she is involved in the band program. Brooke is interested in the Air National Guard after her graduation.

(George) Bud Brand was born in Ashland, Wisconsin and was raised on a farm in Cozy Valley. He graduated from UW-Superior in 1970 and worked for the Duluth Housing Redevelopment Authority for 31 years. He is married with two children and five grandchildren. He has been writing poems for fifty years.

Cecilia Ramón was born in Buenos Aires, Argentina, in 1965. She grew up with the experience of the violence and terror of the 1976-1983 Argentine Dictatorship. Cecilia studied in Buenos Aires with Maria Luisa Manasero and Anselmo Piccoli. She practices painting, sculpture and installation work. She has been living and working in Duluth,MN since 1997. Her work is an inquiry into the nature of the mind, perception, cognition and the root of emotion, like fear and anger, but also joy and equanimity. She is interested in how power affects individuals, society and its relationship to nature. In her practice there is an ongoing meditation on loss, memory and displacement. She explores primarily the language of two materials: wood and paper. She is increasingly searching for an austerity of form and a frugality of means. Wood, as a metaphor of the human body, fragile and strong, subject to gravity and change, allows her to explore visually the body/mind continuum.

Nació en Buenos Aires, Argentina en 1965, Cecilia Ramón creció rodeada de la violencia y el terror de la Dictadura (1976-83). Realizó estudios con María Luisa Manasero y Anselmo Píccoli. Le interesa explorar cómo el poder afecta a los individuos, la sociedad y la relación con la naturaleza. Se dedica a la práctica de la pintura, escultura e intalación. Desde 1997 trabaja en el campo de las artes visuales en Duluth, MN. Su trabajo está inspirado en sus reflexiones acerca de la naturaleza de la mente, la percepción, la cognición y la raíz de las emociones, ya sea miedo, como también alegría y ecuanimidad. En su práctica hay una continua meditación sobre la pérdida, la memoria y el desarraigo. La obra avanza hacia una mayor austeridad formal y hacia una disciplinada frugalidad de medios. Trabaja principalmente con el lenguaje de dos materiales: madera y papel. La madera como metáfora corporal, frágil y fuerte, sujeta a cambios y a la gravedad, le permite explorar visualmente el continuum cuerpo/mente.

Cindy Spillers is an Associate Professor of Communication Sciences and Disorders at UMD for 25+ years. She has a certificate in spiritual direction from the Center for Spiritual Guidance and Leadership, St. Paul, MN. She is an avid gardener and chaser of deer out of the garden. Haiku challenges her to capture multi-layered life experiences in minimalist, metaphorical ways.

Connie Wanek has been writing poems since childhood. She is the author of three books of poetry, most recently *On Speaking Terms* from Copper Canyon Press, and she has been the recipient of several awards, including the Willow Poetry Prize and the Jane Kenyon Poetry Prize. She was named a Witter Bynner Fellow of the Library of Congress by United States Poet Laureate Ted Kooser. In 2009 Wanek was named the George Morrison Artist of the Year, an honor given to a northern Minnesotan for contributions to the arts over many years. She lives in the country outside Duluth, Minnesota, but often finds herself in a green tent somewhere in the Boundary Waters wilderness.

Deborah Gordon Cooper has been writing poetry for twenty years and has worked collaboratively with visual artists, musicians and dancers. She and her husband, Joel, who is a printmaker, have exhibited their collaborative images throughout the Midwest. Deborah has used poetry extensively in her work as a Hospice Chaplain. She co-edited the anthology *Beloved on the Earth: 150 Poems of Grief & Gratitude* (Holy Cow Press, 2009), and she frequently teaches writing classes for those who are grieving the loss of a loved one. She conducts workshops on the interfacing of poetry and spirituality, and mentors inmates at the St. Louis County Jail. Deborah is the author of five collections of poems, most recently *Under the Influence of Lilacs* published by Clover Valley Press, May 2010.

Diane Dinndorf Friebe has been writing all her life — writing a neighborhood newspaper at the age of 9, editing a student newspaper when she taught sixth grade and now writing/editing a professional association newsletter. Diane is retiring to Two Harbors after 15 years in Nebraska and many years all over Minnesota. She has been writing poetry for about eight years. Her work has been published in *Caedmon Song, Emerging Voices* and *Writer's on the Edge*.

Ellie Schoenfeld is a poet native to Duluth, Minnesota. She is the author of books of poetry *The Dark Honey* (Clover Valley Press, 2009), *Screaming Red Gladiolus!* (Poetry Harbor, 1999) and *Difficult Valentines* (Fallow Deer Books, 2004), and her work has been published in an anthology, *The Moon Rolls Out of Our Mouths* (Calyx Press Duluth, 2005), with the four other women in her writing group. Schoenfeld enjoys collaborating with artists of other genres. Her work is featured along with the music of some of her favorite musicians on the CDs *Personal Ad, Almost Through the Rinse Cycle*, and *Taking It Off*. She has worked with area groups Poetry Harbor and Spirit Lake Poetry Series. Though she has thought about it extensively, she has never actually run away with the circus.

Felicia Schneiderhan grew up on the Mississippi River, the daughter of a nun caught by a fisherman. Her short stories and essays appear in various journals and anthologies, including *From the Pews in the Back* and *PMS*. She currently lives in Duluth with her husband and son. This is her first published poem since, oh, probably fifth grade.

Francine Sterle is the author of *Nude in Winter* (Tupelo Press, 2006), an L.A. Times Book of the Year Award finalist, *Every Bird is One Bird* (Editor's Prize, Tupelo Press, 2001), and *The White Bridge* (Poetry Harbor, 1999). Her poems have appeared in such journals as *Poetry International, The North American Review, Ploughshares*, and *Nimrod* and have been anthologized in *Letters to the World, To Sing Along the Way: Minnesota Women Poets From Pre-territorial Days to the Present, The Cancer Poetry Project* and *33 Minnesota Poets*.

Gary Boelhower, PhD is Professor of Theology and Religious Studies at The College of St. Scholastica. He has been writing poetry since grade school. His first book of poetry and stories *Sacred Times, Timeless Seasons* was published in 1986. Recently, Boelhower's poems have been published in the following anthologies: *Beloved on the Earth: 150 Poems of Grief and Gratitude* by Holy Cow! Press, *Trail Guide to the Northland Experience in Prints and Poetry* by Calyx Press Duluth, and *County lines: 87 Minnesota Counties 130 Minnesota Poets* by Loonfeather Press, and the journals *Freshwater Review* and *Willow Review*. His new book *Marrow, Muscle, Flight* will be published by Wildwood River Press October 2011.

Greg Opstad is a retired special education teacher and divides his time between northern Minnesota and Santa Fe, New Mexico. He is a member of Lake Superior Writers. His work has appeared in the *North Coast Review* and in *Trail Guide to the Northland Experience*.

Jan Chronister lives in Maple, Wisconsin and teaches English at Fond du Lac Tribal and Community College. Besides writing, her passions are gardening and reading. Her chapbook *Target Practice* was published by Parallel Press in 2009.

Jane Barrick was born in Duluth and raised in International Falls. She spent 12 years as an editor for Stackpole Books and English teacher in Mechanicsburg,

Pennsylvania. She returned to northern Minnesota in 2008 and is currently an instructor at Rainy River Community College. Jane earned a M. Ed. from Penn State University; her B.A. in English from Gustavus Adolphus College. Her professors there — especially Ann Brady, Deborah Downs-Miers, and Joyce Sutphen — set her on the path toward writing and education. She has never regretted it. Jane and her husband Matthew live in Grand Rapids with their two energetic children: Jonas and Alainna.

Janet Riegle's writing and artwork reflect her fascination with birds. Though her interest in birds blossomed later in life, the seed was planted by her parents, who delighted in the birds visiting the many feeders in their Michigan yard. Music was Janet's first pursuit, teaching flute and performing for many years. When hours of practice grew tedious, she found refuge outdoors. Enthralled with bird song, she sought out the singers, eventually abandoning her flute in favor of spending time with feathered musicians. Janet is the author and illustrator of a children's picture book entitled *Piping Plover Summer*, published by Raven Productions, Inc. in Ely, Minnesota.

Jasmine Baumgart is a student at the University of Wisconsin — Superior (UWS). Her major is English Education because she loves literature and dislikes ignorance. Lake Superior and the beautiful Northwoods stole her away from the Twin Cities where she was raised. Recently she was nominated president of WGSA (Women & Gender Studies Association) at UWS, and she hopes that the group will make a difference in the lives of women within the community. This is her first publication. The poem was written after an enlightening discussion in her feminist theory class. She walked back to her dorm room, sat at her desk, and was then possessed by a furious writing spirit. Jasmine wants this poem to be an empowering declaration of beauty — not beauty of the body, but of the soul. The words are intended to feed the strength of women's hearts and minds, and open the hearts and minds of men.

Jeanine Emmons' home town is Bemidji. She has lived in northern Minnesota all her life except for 3 years in Oregon and 7 years in Minneapolis. Although she started out studying art at Bemidji (then Bemidji State College), she changed her major and transferred to the University in the Twin Cities where she studied sociology and later, nursing. While her creative outlets have been pottery, beading, and drawing, Jeanine has most deeply relied on writing through the years to express herself. She lives with her husband and the trees north of Virginia, MN.

Jeanne C. Maki is a native-born Minnesota Iron Ranger of the "War Baby" generation, a proud member of the Hibbing High School Class of 1961. After 40 years of uprooted city life, she returned to her first home, her maternal grandparents' farm in Idington, where she lives in the present tense, surrounded by the past and its many voices. Jeanne meets regularly with fellow writers who provide her with motivation, encouragement, and a little discipline. Most of her writing is based on observation and memory, as is the piece included here.

Jennifer Derrick is a mostly stay-at-home mother who has a passion for words and language. A part-time freelance writer, she occasionally dabbles in poetry, taking pleasure in the way words can portray emotions and weave stories.

Jill Hinners lives and writes in Duluth, right across the road from Lake Superior. A former bookseller, Jill is still tied to literacy, reading and writing through her service with the Minnesota Reading Corps and her membership in Lake Superior Writers. Her work has been published in *Dust and Fire*, the *Des Moines Register*, and the Iowa Poetry Association's *Lyrical Iowa*. While attending Carleton College in the 1980's (and taking the late Paul Wellstone's Intro to Political Science course), Jill was also published in Carleton's literary journal, *Manuscript*.

Jim Perlman was born and raised in Minneapolis and moved with his family to Duluth in 1988. He is the founding editor and publisher of Holy Cow! Press, www.holycowpress.org. He edited the poetry anthology *Brother Songs: A Male Anthology of Poetry* (1979); with Ed Folsom and Dan Campion, the anthology *Walt Whitman: The Measure of His Song* (1981, 1998); and with Deborah Cooper, Mara Hart, and Pamela Mittlefehldt *Beloved on the Earth: 150 Poems of Grief and Gratitude* (2009). He co-founded The Spirit Lake Poetry Series, and established the Duluth Poet Laureate project in 2005.

Jody J. Bassett lives in Northern Minnesota with her two beautiful children and enjoys hanging out at the lake very much. She loves gardening, cooking, music and writing a bit of poetry thanks to Sheila!!

John McCormick received his M.A. from Miami University in Oxford, Ohio. He has since returned to his home of Superior, Wisconsin where he teaches at UW-Superior, and takes advantage of the tremendous literary and natural wonders of the Northland as much as he is able. His work has appeared on *Arsenic Lobster* and a collaborative chapbook, *Erotic Justice*, from Calyx Press Duluth.

Julie Brooks Barbour received her MFA in Creative Writing at UNC-Greensboro. Her poems have appeared in *New Zoo Poetry Review*, *roger*, *Public Republic*, *UCity Review*, and *PigeonBike*.

Julie Gard is a prose poet who writes off of found objects and unexpected experiences. She is the author of two chapbooks, *Obscura: The Daguerreotype Series* (Finishing Line Press) and *Russia in 17 Objects* (Tiger's Eye Press, forthcoming in Fall 2011). Her prose poetry, nonfiction, and fiction have appeared in *Ekphrasis, Tattoo Highway, Clackamas Literary Review, The MacGuffin*, and a number of other journals and anthologies. You can find her online at juliegard.blogspot. com.

Karen Keenan has a desire for digging into known and not-yet-known ways to use creative processes for practical and artistic expression. She is the grand and great-great grand daughter of Swedish and Norwegian immigrants. The northern Minnesota town of Bemidji was where she experienced her childhood years. In 1977, she and her family moved to Duluth, Minnesota. Karen is a professional educator and musician with interests in pottery, family history and, thanks to Sheila Packa and others, poetry.

Kat Mandeville currently lives in Duluth where she writes and waits tables and occasionally performs.

Kathleen McQuillan is fed by the supportive friendship of other writing women, this tiny (but important) piece of her identity as a creative writer survives, despite the demands and distractions of work, graduate school, family caregiving, and the many challenges of an ordinary day in Cook, Minnesota. When time is set aside to create, recollect and record images and insights, she grows in her relationship with self, her world and her most intimate companions on this journey through Life. The joy and discovery never fail to surprise her.

Kim Sisto-Robinson's website is called myinnerchick.com which is dedicated to her sister, Kay, who was murdered on May 26, 2010. Kim writes about domestic violence and women's issues. "I adore the women of the Beat Generation such as Plath, Sexton & Jong. These delectable creatures are the reason I write today. I am an obsessive blogger & devourer of poetry."

Kyle Elden is first and foremost the mother of a beautiful six year old girl Stella Marais. Additionally, she is a child protection social worker at Saint Louis County and Yoga Instructor at Yoga North. She loves spending time in nature, playing on the beach of Park Point, traveling, running, theology, laughing out loud as much as possible, and reading and writing. She writes as a way to witness, process, and understand life — both the difficult to bear and the astonishingly beautiful and blessed.

Laura Krueger-Kochmann holds a bachelor of arts degree in English and creative writing from St. Cloud State University and a master of arts degree in English from the University of Minnesota Duluth. She loves to write poetry and finds inspiration in memories, canoe trips, and bedtime stories. Laura has spent most of her life in Wisconsin and Minnesota and enjoys living in Duluth with her husband, Todd, and her daughter, Cordelia.

Leah Rogne, PhD, of Orr and Mankato, Minnesota, is Associate Professor of Sociology at Minnesota State University, Mankato. She teaches Sociology of Death, Applied Sociology, Program Planning, and Nursing Home Administration; and supervises internships for Gerontology and Sociology. Her research is on long-term peace activists, culture change in long-term care, and social insurance and the privatization debate. Rogne was co-editor of *Social Insurance and Social Justice: Social Security, Medicare, and the Campaign against Entitlements* (Springer 2009). She is a native of North Dakota.

Linda LeGarde Grover is Bois Forte Ojibwe from northern Minnesota and an Associate Professor in the Department of American Indian Studies at the University of Minnesota Duluth. Her chapbook *THE.INDIAN.AT.INDIAN.SCHOOL* was the 2008 selection of the University of Arkansas at Little Rock Sequoyah Research Center Native Writers Series. Her manuscript "The Road Back to Sweetgrass" received the Native Writers Circle of the Americas 2008 First Book Award, and her book *The Dance Boots*, which was published in September 2010 has received the Flannery O'Connor Award for Short Fiction. Her research interests include the 20th century American Indian experience as well as Indian education, particularly the boarding school experience and its effects on traditional education and Native families and communities.

Linda M. Johnson is a small-town girl at heart from Esko, MN. Her poetry and short stories can be found in various publications. In 2010 she was thrilled to win first place in the *Northwoods Woman* fiction contest and excited to see her first memoir piece published. She savors small pleasures like dark chocolate and a good cup of coffee. If you ask her advice she'd say read poetry just for fun.

Lisa Poje Angelos, originally from Milwaukee, now works for Minnesota DNR and lives along Superior's North Shore with her husband Peter. Although she pursued science degrees including a B.S. in Geography from Penn State and an M.S. in Environmental Science from Indiana University, her ever-eclectic personality always allows room for the liberal arts. Her writing has been published in *Cabin Life*, *Friends of Acadia Journal*, *Dust and Fire* and in collaborative anthologies and exhibitions by Calyx Press Duluth and Crossings at Carnegie. She is happiest in the woods, in the company of animals, traveling, or cooking for friends and family.

Liz Minette has been writing for about 10 years. Some of her writing topics cover animals, nature, transitions. Some publication credits include *Abbey*, *Nerve Cowboy*, *Earth's Daughters*, *Many Mountains Moving*, among others. She works in Duluth at a community access television station and lives and writes out of Esko, Minnesota.

Loree Miltich notes that her most satisfying creative work has been collaborative, working with visual artists Vernal Bogren-Swift, Gendron Jensen, and now with poet, Susan Hawkinson on the "Migration" project. Inspired by Jackie Solem's photography, Loree's "voice" is in the column on the right and Susan's is on the left. However, the poem is intended to be read across columns as a "double-voiced" poem. Loree's writing has appeared in publications such as *The Georgia Review* and *To Topio: Poetry International*. She lives north of Grand Rapids with her family, and teaches at Union Institute & University.

Lynda Ferguson is a writer, illustrator, and theater costumer in the process of developing a street theater company called Road Kill Theater and Design. She is also currently working with the Arrowhead Alliance of Artists With Disabilities (AAAWD) on the 2011 Duluth MN Disability Mural Project, and has a children's book, *Golly, Gee, and Um*, in progress.

Lynn Fena lives and writes in northern Minnesota where she has unexpectedly, and mostly contentedly, lived throughout her life. Beginning as a teen poet, her devotion to the writer's life has waxed and waned over time. She writes now to know and be known, to reveal beauty in everyday experience and to explore the connection between emotion and place.

Maggie Kazel is a mom, a writer, and manages two youth service programs in Duluth. She is midwestern by roots and by choice, with east coast, west coast and southern years gathered in between.

Marce Wood is a visual artist who spends her time between Duluth and Grand Marais. She writes tiny poems in order to be attentive to what each day brings.

Marie Zhuikov is an award-winning writer specializing in environmental and medical topics. She has produced hundreds of articles and publications. Her poems have appeared in several anthologies and community projects and she is a member of the speculative fiction writers' group through Lake Superior Writers. Her first novel, an eco-mystic romance, will be coming out in 2011 from North Star Press. Zhuikov has a BA in science journalism and an MA in public health journalism. She currently works as an environmental project administrator for the St. Louis River Alliance in Duluth, Minn.

Margaret Veeder lives on Rainy Lake near International Falls in the far northern reaches of Minnesota. Raised in Milwaukee, WI, she graduated from the University of Wisconsin-Madison with a degree in Journalism, and moved to International Falls three decades ago to accept a position as a newspaper reporter. She's been there ever since, now employed in communications and marketing for a financial institution. She enjoys travel, reading, classic rock concerts, genealogy, cooking and planning family occasions with her husband, two sons and their spouses and two grandchildren. Her car will veer to the side of the road to visit an old church, an old cemetery, an old friend, or a child's lemonade stand. She writes about family life, life on the border, generational influences and grandparenting from a distance.

Mark Maire has lived in Duluth for most of his adult life. He is a reference librarian at the public library. His poetry has appeared most recently in *The Minnetonka Review*, and is forthcoming in *Slant: A Journal of Poetry*.

Michelle Matthees is the author of three poetry chapbooks, *Served, Outside*, and

Junket, all published by Press This! Michelle has received grants, awards and fellowships from the Minnesota State Arts Board, the Arrowhead Regional Artists Council, the Jerome Foundation, and Associated Writing Programs, and she was also a 2009 Jerome/ SASE Emerging Writer. Her poems have appeared in *The Bloomsbury Review, Hayden's Ferry Review, PANK, The Bellingham Review, Cerise Press*, and in numerous other journals. She lives in Duluth, Minnesota.

Micky McGilligan is a poetry addict that has attended workshops and classes with many of her favorite authors and writers. She has learned much from these experiences and has made friends who have enriched her life as well as her writing. She has published poetry and essays for over 30 years in publications such as *Loonfeather, North Coast Review*, both Poetry Harbor regional anthologies, *Mother Earth News*, has done translations from Spanish poetry in *Kalliope*, and has won awards from The Depot's Lake Superior Writer's Series, Poetry Project II, Poetry Harbor, and spent two weeks at the juried Norcroft Women's Retreat.

Molly Tillotson uses sculpture and writing to interpret memories and current life in the woods north of Lake Superior. She is fascinated with how senses and memory interact such that we can be transported to another place and time by the simplest experience.

Moriah Erickson resides in Duluth, MN with her husband, 7 children, and one silent plott hound. She works part time as a respiratory therapist, and is currently pursuing a MFA in poetry from Fairfield University. She has had multiple poems and stories published in journals including *Permafrost, Common Ground Review, Rosebud* and others. She won the 2010 Frances Kahn Memorial Prize for poetry and placed 2nd in the 2010 William Stafford Poetry Contest. She enjoys laundry and cooking for mass consumption.

Nance O'Brien is a Duluth native who packed her bags to leave the Zenith City at the age of nine and finally caught a ride west nine years later. After adventures and misadventures in Montana, Mexico, and Spain, she returned home to teach at her alma mater. She has taught Spanish to teenagers since 1982.

Pamela Mittlefehldt is a poet and fiddler who lives in Duluth. She is co-editor of *Beloved on the Earth: 150 Poems of Grief and Gratitude*, and is currently writing a mystery and working on a book about the meaning of place.

Peggy Trojan, retired to the north Wisconsin woods with her husband. Member of Wisconsin Fellowship of Poets. Published in *Dust and Fire, Wilda Morris Challenge, WFOP* calendars, *Talking Stick, Echoes, Finnish American Reporter*.

Penny Perry grew up on a farm in Spooner, WI and has lived, and operated a frame shop, in Duluth, MN for over 30 years. She has the benefit of many gracious and impelling teachers. Her poems come from a place betwixt daydreaming and paying attention.

Rocky Kiukanpi is a Lakota word for "Makes Room For Them." He was born on the Rosebud reservation in South Dakota, graduated in Minnesota. discovered writing while being in the USMC stationed in Hawaii, moved to Duluth, met his wife Tracey and had three children. Rocky is now living on the north shore of Lake Superior near the French River.

Ryan Vine's poems appear widely. He is Assistant Professor and Rose Warner Professor of English at the College of St. Scholastica in Duluth, Minnesota.

Ryan W. Keller is from the small community of Mora, MN, where he was raised on a hobby farm. Ryan attended the University of Minnesota Duluth and is a proud alumni still living in Duluth. Ryan recently married and is pursuing a career caring for adults with persistent mental illness. A writer still discovering his style, Ryan hopes this anthology will be the first of many publications.

Sheila Packa lives in northern Minnesota near Lake Superior. She has three books of poems, *The Mother Tongue* (Calyx Press Duluth, 2007), *Echo & Lightning*, and *Cloud Birds* (both Wildwood River Press, 2010 and 2011). *Echo & Lightning* received a 2011 Golden Crown Award for Poetry. Her poems have been in several anthologies, including *Good Poems American Places* (Viking Penguin, 2011), *Finnish-North American Literature in English* (Mellen Press, 2009), *Beloved of the Earth: 150 Poems of Grief and Gratitude* (Holy Cow! Press ©2009) and *To Sing Along the Way: Minnesota Women Poets from Pre-Territorial Days to the Present* (New Rivers Press, ©2006). She has received two Arrowhead Regional Arts Council fellowships for poetry, an ARAC Career Opportunity grant (2007), two Loft McKnight Awards, (poetry 1986 and prose 1996) a Loft Mentor Award in poetry (1995), and a Community Arts Learning Grant (2010). She is the poet laureate of Duluth, 2010-2012. More information is at www.sheilapacka.com.

Shelley Getten moved from Minnetonka to Two Harbors, Minnesota in 2008. Over the years she has been published in many anthologies and magazines including *Minnesota Monthly, Rag Mag, Sidewalks* and the *Minnesota Poetry Calendar*. She has edited two anthologies: *Breast Works* (to date unpublished) and *Grounds for Peace*. Her poetry chapbook, *Agates*, was published in 2005 by Finishing Line Press. Shelley has recently been creating block print art, which can be found at Northwoods Pioneer Gallery in Castle Danger. She lives with her husband, Brien, son, Devin and daughter, Brighid, in a log cabin on the Knife River. She feels these last few years have helped her develop her understanding and acceptance of the transitory quality of life.

Sherry Rovig is known by many for her work designing equipment for people with disabilities. A number of her designs have received patents and are sold online and in stores. Others know her as a volunteer fire fighter, first responder, and creator of the mouth-watering spaghetti sauce for the annual Harvest Dinner benefit. Her creative energy is channeled to music, writing, and building anything from a sustainable homestead to giant snow sculptures. Her poetry and essays have been published in *Dust and Fire*, in a WDSE Cookbook, and in community garden newsletters, and on websites. She lives in the country near Lake Superior.

Stephanie Kessler wrote her first poem at age 14, which was published when she was 16. She loves writing poetry and its ability to soothe and free the soul through written words. The poem "Lightning" was written after she discovered her love of reading to her own children and realized her childhood had so few memories of books. Stephanie has Bachelor's and Master's degrees in Geography/Water Resources. She works for the Federal Emergency Management Agency intermittently and consults as an Event Planner, but her favorite job is homeschooling her son and daughter.

Susan Hawkinson flew with her father in a four-passenger Cessna 182 from the time she was ten years old until her father quit flying a few years before his death. On one trip her father forgot the navigational charts, and they followed the highways and read the names of the towns on watertowers all the way from Grand Rapids, Minnesota, to Cedar Falls, Iowa. Her father was a road contractor. Hawkinson is a co-author, along with Warren Jewett, of *Timber Connections: The Joyce Lumber Story*, a 2004 Minnesota Book Award finalist.

Susan Niemela Vollmer grew up in Ely, and later lived near Duluth for many years. She is a writer and a former teacher of gifted and talented students who lives in Rice Lake, Wisconsin with her husband. Her work has appeared in *Minnesota Monthly, North Coast Review, Finnish American Reporter, Lake Country Journal, The Talking Stick, Dust and Fire, Between Stone and Flesh*, and other publications.

Tera Freese began writing poetry at age eleven when she received a blank book as a gift from her godmother. She has always sought out wild, quiet places to tap into the source of all poems. Her work has been published in *Calliope, North Coast Review* and *Avocet*. She self-published a collection with three other poets titled *The Stones In Her Pocket*. She lives in the woods of northeastern Minnesota with her husband, Paul and two daughters, Maria and Scarlet. She is trying to teach herself to live simply, mindfully and joyfully.

Teresa Alto teaches English at Itasca Community College in Grand Rapids. Like many English majors, she tried her hand at a range of communication jobs — ACT test writer and editor, book editor, public relations writer, freelance editor — before finding her home as a community college English instructor. What she values about Itasca is that it provides the full college experience and education while creating community. Despite her background, writing poetry is fairly new for Teresa. This year, for the first time ever, she wrote each of her parents a poem for Mother's Day and Father's Day respectively. She still loves to bike.

Teresa Boyle Falsani grew up in Portland, Maine and moved Duluth, Minnesota with her husband in 1973. A mother of two, she enjoyed her careers as writer/creative director at an advertising agency and as an English teacher. Falsani is a two-time winner of Lake Superior Writers' Contests for her poetry and drama. Her writing appears in *Dust and Fire, Beloved on the Earth: 150 Poems of Grief and Gratitude, Trail Guide to the Northland Experience in Prints and Poetry*, and several other anthologies and journals.

Terry S. Dunham has a BFA in drawing and is a writer, photographer, gardener and the parent of a graduate student. She has worked in development, grant writing and marketing since moving to Duluth 10 years ago. She participates in several writing groups and serves as co-chair of the Lake Superior Writers board of directors. Another flash fiction piece is published at minnesotaartists.net. Terry lives with her husband in Chester Park.

Theresa O'Halloran-Johnson is a social worker by trade, craft and passion. She has three children, none of whom are juveniles any more. She is married to a man who lives 250 miles away. Theresa sometimes writes recipes, which are more like dialogues than recipes. She loves to read and write, but sometimes writing is more difficult than she cares to explain.

Tina Higgins graduated from the MFA program in Creative Writing from Hamline University in St. Paul. She is honored to have worked with Sheila O'Connor, Deborah Keenan, Susan Power, Anne Pancake and James Moore. Although Tina focused on fiction for her final thesis project, she studied both poetry and fiction side-by-side throughout graduate school — fascinated by the symbiotic relationship between genres. Her fiction can be read at www.brinklit.com and www.furnacereview.com. Tina lives in Duluth with music, nature, friends, laughter, love and Henry the Dog.

Yvonne Rutford lives near Duluth and writes poetry and prose inspired primarily by the landscape of northern Minnesota, and by her dogs. Her poetry collection *This Fragile Nest* was published in 2009, and her essay "Learning to Fly" was recently published in the *Clockhouse Review*. Yvonne earned an MFA in creative writing from Goddard College, Vermont, and teaches writing at the University of Wisconsin–Superior.

SOURCES AND PERMISSIONS

"Long Nights" and "The Midwife" are from *Hartley Field.* Copyright ©2002 by Connie Wanek. Used by permission of The Permissions Company, Inc., on behalf of Holy Cow! Press, www.holycowpress.org

"Honey" and "Pumpkin" are from *On Speaking Terms.* Copyright ©2010 by Connie Wanek. Used by permission of The Permissions Company, Inc., on behalf of Copper Canyon Press, www.coppercanyonpress.org

"Target Practice" by Jan Chronister is from *Target Practice,* Parallel Press, Copyright ©2009 by the Board of Regents of the University of Wisconsin System. Used by permission from Parallel Press. www.parallelpress.library.wisc.edu

"Flowering" is from *Common Threads*, Talking Stick, Volume 18. Copyright ©2009 by Jan Chronister.

"Two Days" is from *UCityReview.* Copyright ©2011 by Julie Brooks Barbour. www.ucityreview.com/2_Barbour_Julie_Brooks.html

"Telephone Wire" is from *Tiger's Eye Journal* Spring 2011. Copyright ©2011 by Julie Gard. This poem is forthcoming in the chapbook, *Russia in 17 Objects*, Tiger's Eye Press, 2011.

"Skipping to Middle Chapters for Graphic Description" is from *Prick of the Spindle.* Copyright ©2009 by Kat Mandeville. www.prickofthespindle.com/poetry/3.4/mandeville/skipping_to_middle.htm

"Fishing" is from *The Oak*, Fall 2009. Copyright ©2009 by Moriah Erickson.

"Appearances," "Between Us," "Casting Off" and "Litany on the Beach" are from *Marrow, Muscle, Flight,* Wildwood River Press. Copyright ©2011 by Gary Boelhower.

"What Ward Prefers" is from *The American Poetry Review.* Copyright ©2010 by Ryan Vine. www.aprweb.org/issue/marchapril-2010

"Snowbank Sherpa" is from *The Cortland Review* August 2009. Copyright ©2010 by Ryan Vine. www.cortlandreview.com/issue/44/vine.html

"Ward's Rule 5" appeared in the *Minneapolis Star Tribune,* June 3, 2011. Copyright ©2011 by Ryan Vine. www.startribune.com/lifestyle/123118728.html

"Unbidden" is from *The Tenth Annual Poet Artist Collaboration*, Crossings at Carn-

INDEX OF FIRST LINES

182

INDEX BY LAST NAMES